Living With Catherine McAuley

Ulana M. Bochan

iUniverse, Inc.
New York   Bloomington

Living With Catherine McAuley

The views expressed in this work are solely those of the author and do not necessarily reflect the views of the publisher, and the publisher hereby disclaims any responsibility for them.

iUniverse books may be ordered through booksellers or by contacting:

iUniverse
1663 Liberty Drive
Bloomington, IN 47403
www.iuniverse.com
1-800-Authors (1-800-288-4677)

Because of the dynamic nature of the Internet, any Web addresses or links contained in this book may have changed since publication and may no longer be valid.

ISBN: 978-1-4502-4617-0 (sc)
ISBN: 978-1-4502-4772-6 (ebk)

Printed in the United States of America

iUniverse rev. date: 9/7/2010

DEDICATION

To

Elyse Juliana Bochan, my beautiful five-year old grandchild, whose sensitivity to her world already promises blossoms of compassion.

And to

The loving memory of my mother, Maria Kramarczuk, who practiced the gift of unconditional love.

ACKNOWLEDGMENTS

I stand in gratitude to Mary C. Sullivan, RSM, a member of the Rochester, New York regional community of the Institute of the Sisters of Mercy of the Americas, for her valuable assistance in furthering this project.

A thank you to my husband, Bohdan, for his support and encouragement.

Special recognition to Danylo Michael Bochan for designing the artistic cover.

Contents

FORWORD

Living With Catherine McAuley provides an examination of a life shepherded by Catherine McAuley. Divided into four major parts, it shows a journey from the past to the present. **Part I** contains significant signposts that spell out the trajectory of one life. My journey from the past to the present shows the workings of a free will guided by Providence that ultimately leads to a teaching ministry at a Mercy school, Assumption High School in Louisville, Kentucky. It is written for the purpose of inviting everyone who reads it to examine the patterns that have led to the moment of now, so that he/she can recognize God's presence and shape a clearer view of not only personal direction but also, earthly work yet to be accomplished.

Part II deals with Mercy values of humility, compassion and unconditional love – the basics of the Mercy charism as exemplified by Catherine McAuley. This section is a continuation of my journey, specifying my initiation into Catherine's way of life within my teaching ministry. This reflective view encapsulates the gradual growth and understanding of how these practiced values of humility, compassion and love can spiritually enrich both the student and the teacher. In my opinion, making Catherine's values inherent in any ministry encourages the "unbelievable" to happen. Not only has Catherine created "magic" in my life, but she has also transformed my approach to it. She has engendered an indisputable identity that fortifies my strengths and gives direction to the "now" of my life.

Part III is a pedagogical approach that incorporates Catherine's values on a daily basis. In this type of classroom atmosphere, Catherine becomes a "living spirit", helping students go beyond the facts into a realm of positive self-actualization. Respect for one another becomes a staple in the classroom. It is the base upon which all the other values are built. This section encourages the reader to examine pedagogical strategies that work while building a strong communal bond between students and teacher. The culmination of this type of Catherine-based knowledge has sprouted a recognition of what unconditional love might mean in interactions with others. Unconditional love denotes a Christian love where one would give one's life for the betterment of others – just as Jesus did. However, in view of Catherine's charism, I believe giving one's life can take on a metaphorical meaning: Christian servanthood where the "self" lovingly ministers to the needs of others.

Part IV: Catherine McAuley Moments can become a way of life when someone has been immersed into the Mercy tradition or simply wishes to reinforce Mercy values. This Part defines a Catherine Moment: a reciprocal giving and receiving. It is the carrying on of a legacy, a commitment, to live a life of Mercy where compassion lights the darkest room. In today's problem-ridden world where "man's inhumanity to man" often reigns, one ordinary individual "living with Catherine McAuley" can make a Mercy difference. All of us can be merciful transporters of hope. Since life is categorized by moments, why not make them Mercy ones? An invitation to create a "living spirit" in our lives is an invitation to share our loving moments with our neighbor. Who is our neighbor? Everyone we meet on the path of life.

INTRODUCTION

Why Catherine McAuley?

Although Catherine McAuley was born September 29, 1778 and died November 11, 1841, the spirit of her legacy continues into today, affecting both religious and lay people. Because the universality of her beliefs is timeless, her charism of mercy has taken fire throughout the world. It has reached my corner of the world, bringing a kindling into my soul as I read about her life and mission and reflected on my 23 years of teaching ministry at a Mercy school.

On my journey in life, I have encountered many people who have influenced my life. Some, I could credit immediately as creative, positive signposts in my life; others have taken on a particular significance through introspective recollections. Catherine McAuley's effect on my life emerged in my first year of retirement as I reflected back on the maze-like path my life had taken. Some of Catherine McAuley's personal signposts signaled the steps in my own life journey.

From early on, Catherine experienced an emotional and spiritual orphanhood, leading her to a sole reliance on God's providence. Her father, James McGauley, died when she was only five years old; her mother passed away in 1798 when she was 20. Because of these early deaths,

Catherine was forced to move from one family to another. She first lived in the home of William Armstrong where her sister and brother were. At the Armstrongs, she experienced trials of faith, yet she remained stalwart in her Catholic beliefs. Although she suffered spiritually as her faith was ridiculed, she never wavered from it. Catherine's sole reliance on God's providence helped me to recognize God's workings in my life.

In 1803, an opportunity presented itself to Catherine to move in with the Callaghans as a companion to Mrs. Callaghan. There she was allowed to follow her Catholic beliefs; eventually by her exemplary demeanor, she became responsible for the conversion of both Callaghans to Catholicism. She selflessly ministered to their physical and spiritual needs for a total of 19 years. With Mrs. Callaghan's death in 1819 and her husband's in 1822, Catherine became the Callaghans' "sole residuary legatee" (Sullivan, *Catherine McAuley* 10). Declining a marriage proposal and becoming a wealthy heiress at 43, Catherine could have easily used the enormous inheritance for her own personal needs; instead, she had a vision to construct a home on Baggot Street to shelter the underprivileged women in the area. On September 24, 1827, her vision became a reality as she witnessed the official opening of the house on Baggot Street "as a school for the education of poor young girls and as a residence for homeless girls and women" (11). These selfless, brave acts of hers became my indicators that I needed to turn outward, to be less introverted and self-absorbed.

Catherine's original intent with Baggot Street was simply to help the impoverished. She never envisioned forming a religious order; eventually, however, as more lay women joined her in her mission, it began to take on religious ramifications; she finally consented to its formation as a religious order. On December 12, 1831, Catherine, Mary Ann Doyle and Mary Elizabeth Harley professed their vows and established "the Congregation called the Sisters of Mercy"

(13). This congregation inflamed by the Mercy charism had its purpose to bring "education to poor and wretched Girls who could not otherwise procure or obtain it…, [to] lodge poor Servant-girls" who were unemployed, and "[to] visit the Hospitals and there serve and assist the sick" (Sullivan, *Correspondence* 43). All of these works of Mercy were to be patterned after the example of Jesus. Catherine states in the Rule and Constitutions of the Religious Sister of Mercy that "[in] undertaking [the] duty of instructing the poor, the Sisters…shall animate their zeal and fervor by the example of their Divine Master Jesus Christ…" (Sullivan, *Catherine McAuley* 295*)*. Furthermore, in naming the order as Sisters of Mercy, this newly formed Congregation paid tribute to the Blessed Virgin "regarding her as their Mother, and the great Model they are obliged to imitate…" (311).

Dedication to the Blessed Mother and faithfulness in following the cross of Christ became the Mercy Call that echoed throughout the world, creating new houses of Mercy not only in Ireland, England, but also extending to the United States and beyond. Roland Burke Savage emphasizes the vastness of this spread in *Catherine McAuley:The First Sister of Mercy:* "The ten short years of her own religious life were but the seeding-time; it was only after her death that the full fruitfulness of her life began to show itself. At the time of her death there were little more than 100 Sisters of Mercy; fifteen years later there were 3,000…one hundred years later there were 23,000" (qtd. in Burns and Carney 14). In performing ordinary actions in an extraordinary way, Catherine created a legacy and legion of followers who, in their own way, tried to follow her example either as a Mercy religious or as a lay person dedicated to the same ideals. Being immersed in the Mercy tradition as a teacher, I realized how Catherine's solid Christian values became a way of life for me, influencing my teaching style as well as my interaction with others.

The Foundress, Catherine McAuley, was God-driven to live a life of Mercy, placing her total trust in Divine Providence. She was an amazing individual whose advice on ordinary actions has repercussions for all of us even today: In Chapter 5: Of the Perfection of Ordinary Actions in the Rule and Constitutions, she states a simple but astute truth that can pave the way to spiritual self knowledge: "The perfection of the religious soul depends, not so much on doing extraordinary actions, as on doing extraordinarily well the ordinary actions and exercises of every day" (Sullivan, *Catherine McAuley* 300). Her extraordinary persona is very well summarized by Regan and Keiss in *Tender Courage* based on her extant letters:

> [Catherine McAuley] the woman writing to keep all foundations abreast of one another is affectionate, tender, funny, graceful, confiding, wise. The woman of business is direct, concise, well-bred. The woman of the Church writing to bishops and priests is candid, cordial, obedient, and dignified. The woman who is Superior writing to censure is pained, sandwiching reproof between affectionate greetings and long newscasts to assure it is the deed not the doer that draws her ire. (43)

The woman, Catherine McAuley, was and still is a disciple of Christ in the minds of her followers. For me, Catherine McAuley is a role model of what a Christian should strive to be. I have been affected substantially by her sense of humility, compassion and unconditional love for all human beings, especially, the ones condemned by societal standards. She was a woman of personal sacrifices. Her deeds of servant-like love engendered and nurtured throughout her basically short life span of 63 years, overpowered temporal time. Catherine's impact on a way of life is still strongly in existence today, 169 years after her death.

Through my teaching ministry, I have witnessed her living presence through relying on God's providential hand that led me to working in a Mercy school. There was a tremendous amount that I needed to learn and re-shape in my life to better understand human need. Catherine McAuley has been my invisible role model, making her presence known to me through the needs of my students and colleagues. For me, her influence has not stopped with my teaching ministry in the classroom but continues with a commitment to minister to others, sharing what I have learned in the context of Mercy values.

My journey with Catherine McAuley under God's Providence is a journey anyone can make. It is based on selected universal values; it is a placing of trust in a way of life that mirrors a Christian approach. Whether a journey is "Living with Catherine McAuley", or with any other spiritual mentor, it becomes one well worth pursuing because it creates a purpose in doing "the ordinary, extraordinarily well" as Catherine McAuley would say. Following the path of Christianity can bring each one of us closer to our God-intended self. I have found that in the complexity of modern chaos, peace will reign when guided by the beautiful simplicity of Jesus' statement: "Love one another" (John 16:17). This universal mandate can help spread unconditional love, creating a purposeful existence – for when unconditional love is present, conditioned hate is absent.

Part I: Signposts

How has Catherine influenced my life so that I can say, "I have lived with Catherine McAuley"? Can she become an active presence in a life, especially a secular life? We all search for a purpose in life, at all ages. Reflection nags at us from time to time but seems to become more predominant in "the twilight years". It is my hope that in sharing my introspective views with all educators, especially, the younger generation, I will encourage them to look at their lives in the present moment, and connect their own past for the purpose of illuminating the present. In the present moment lies our purpose, not only as educators, but also as human beings.

So, how has Catherine become my spiritual mentor and how did the signposts in my life lead to this moment of recognition? I can only recognize Catherine's gift to me through connecting signposts of the past with today's epiphany of understanding that has led me to a spiritual readiness to minister to others.

Allow me to take you on my journey and explain the signposts that will eventually point to "living with" Catherine McAuley and accepting her mission of mercy with love. These signposts occurred on their own, set up, not by me, but by God. In fact, many times I tried to change direction, prayed for direction and ended up going in an unforeseen way. Many may argue that coincidences happen to everyone and are just that, "coincidences". But when too many coincidences are thrown in one's way and it becomes a way of life, they defy their own definition. Gaps of reason ask to be filled and when reason fails, faith must come in.

Just as all human journeys begin, mine began with my birth in the Ukraine. As a newborn, I was not expected to live, but despite the odds of an incurable digestive disorder, I survived. My dad's words at that point in time consisted of a plea to God: "Please let her live or just let her die." Miraculously, I survived. In 1943 when I was two years old, World War II reached our quiet village. At two, I do not remember much but somehow, traumatic experiences implanted themselves into my subconscious later to be filled in with details by my parents. The German soldiers had entered our peaceful village with guns, looking for any Jewish people that might be sheltered within our homes. In haste, my mother, father and brother fled from the home, leaving behind a squalling two year old. Evidently, as the story goes, I was not physically harmed – just abandoned. Somehow, I ended up in my aunt's home, crying uncontrollably, uttering incoherent words. Several tortuous hours later, after the soldiers had gone, I was reunited with my parents.

Although the German soldiers terrified us, we were more afraid of the prevalent communism enveloping our country. Many attempted an exodus to avoid communism which was a threat to core values, especially religion. My parents were among them. We fled in a horse and buggy. This distinct childhood memory was lodged in my subconscious and nightmared thereafter: the unbearable noise of human suffering, a sky eerily lit up like an explosion of fireworks, with ear deafening bombs that could not silence the high pitched cacophonous neighing of horses. The journey was perilous with life and death intermingling. My two-year-old eyes must have registered a chaotic world composed of fear and doubt. Huddled as a family, we journeyed on.

My father was practical; my mother very religious. She clutched an icon of the Blessed Virgin, a simple picture, and incessantly prayed. Miraculous deliverances from death occurred as she sheltered us with her body in a ravine because of low flying bombers. Her acts of heroism to save her children on this road to freedom were many and have not been recorded anywhere, except in the hearts of my brother and me.

From my mother, I learned early on to rely solely on God, an echo of Catherine who said in one of her letters to Sister M. Angela Dunne: "Put your whole confidence in God" (Sullivan, *Correspondence* 113). Skeptics may label our survival as luck due to coincidences. Luck? Coincidences? They are too fleeting, too unpredictable. No, an ingrained, unwavering faith in the Mercy of God gave us purpose to persevere. Faith defies all human definition. Faith once established can be debated but cannot be cancelled by human reason. Our early trials and tribulations through many countries eventually led us to a harbor of safety - to no other land than the United States of America.

My perilous journey, from a safe homeland where we experienced wealth, to the dregs of poverty in Germany, to the American dream, echoes for me part of Catherine's early life experience. She went from a secure, loving home, to an experience of dire poverty with the Conways, to adapting to a completely new environment as an adopted daughter of the Callaghans (Burns and Carney 18-19). However, this pilgrim existence eventually brought her to her purpose in life - to minister to the needy.

My real American journey began in Minnesota in 1949. A parish sponsored our family, covering the cost of our emigration from Germany to the U.S. As I child in Germany, I had become acquainted with American generosity. I remember waiting in line to get a Red Cross package of pencils, toothbrushes and other useful items. Those days became my understanding of Christmas. I recall the long lines with my parents to get bread and milk: white bread and milk if you had children; otherwise, dark bread. In my childlike way, I began to understand the meaning of compassion - someone understood our need; someone cared and didn't wait for a thank you. I believe compassion followed me like a shadow that eventually concretized into a way of life. Catherine personally knew what it meant to be destitute; therefore, Catherine knew that compassion should grow into mercy towards others. "Awareness that her charism, her gift for others, was mercy began to be an explicit consciousness for Catherine…" (Regan and Keiss 46).

In 1949, my parents enrolled me in a Catholic grade school which was run by Benedictine sisters who tried their hardest to acclimate me by changing my name to Juliana to help me seem more Americanized and to be named after a saint. However, this change of name simply reinforced my lack of identity, creating a duality within me. (I was Juliana until my college days, and then I legally reverted back to my birth name.) I started first grade knowing no English. My peers thought that, to use a euphemism, I was low on the scale of intelligence. I was a very shy, introverted child and suffered internally from their ostracism. However, by the end of grade one, the teacher recommended that I skip second grade. I did. From then on, my grade school education progressed rather normally. What I learned from this experience was to always look out for and stand up for anyone who does not fit in. It was an invaluable lesson that served me well in the formation of compassion that prepared me for an acceptance of diversity.

When it came time for high school, I planned on going to a public school because the elite all-girls Catholic school was exceedingly expensive. We were highly encouraged as eighth graders to just take the entrance test regardless of our destination. It was rumored to be a "tough" test with homogeneous groupings. I took the test. I had nothing to lose. Unexpectedly,

I scored very high on the entrance exam which made me a desirable candidate. My parents then decided to make more sacrifices to send me to this exclusive all-girls high school. Here, I received an excellent education from which I would later draw selectively when teaching in a Mercy school. Again, I was being prepared by Providence in a direction that was totally unimaginable at this point in time. Being a teacher had never crossed my mind. I had been taking all kinds of lessons - music, dance, voice, modeling - and had grand visions of an applauded future. What I didn't realize until just recently was that I would eventually be adapting this whole agenda to teaching the mission set out by Catherine McAuley.

In every life, there are turbulent years that test one's value system. For me, college was one of them. In choosing to further my education, I decided on the University of Minnesota. Having taken equivalent coursework to our AP standards now, and scoring well on the required national qualifying exam, I was accepted into the University. My experiences at the University of Minnesota from 1959 to 1963 took me in multiple directions. I was basically hit with a secular outlook that permeated my whole being. Freedom of thought and action challenged my hard-core identity creating a duality within me. Here again, I'm reminded of the spiritual duality Catherine faced when living with the Armstrongs and being subjected to ridicule of her Catholic faith. Burns and Carney state that Catholics were often "viewed…as generally wallowing in poverty, superstition, and bad taste….In the face of steady, often scornful proselytizing, Catherine regretted that her own lack of education prevented her from effectively defending the faith that she held with such conviction" (18). Although I may have undergone some of the anguish that Catherine did, I have to say that mine was self-made. I became somewhat arrogant about my faith. It seemed in vogue to argue about the existence of God, so I did. Intellectual reasoning became my tool for winning - a game. Pride within me swelled. The Bible states that "The beginning of pride is man's stubborness in withdrawing his heart from his Maker" (Sirach 10:12). I was withdrawing from my foundation but didn't realize this until senior year. It was then that I started a process of self-examination that lasted intensively for the next two years. In the meantime, college became a four year desperate search: Freshman year, I was going into a medical field; Sophomore year, into social work; Junior year, basically, nowhere; Senior year, I decided if I wanted to graduate I needed to pack the year with a solid goal that I could realistically reach. I decided to declare an English major, cramming in all the courses needed to graduate. This intellectual scrambling put faith on hold. It caused an indecisiveness that led to seriously doubting my spiritual convictions. Arrogance coupled with a secular milieu was wiping out everything I had hitherto believed to be unquestionable. My paradigm had shifted. The answer to the maze I had created pointed to only one talisman - God - but how to reach Him? It was a long way back but I knew that without God, I would lead a vacuous existence. I read spiritual works, I talked to priests, I journaled, I prayed and prayed. I even considered becoming a nun. I was trying to go from one extreme to the other. Balance was yet to be found. However, prayer became a constant in my life. By that I mean, a constant mental effort to tell my Heavenly Friend where I was at and ask for help. I felt a schism in my soul which led to the feeling of abandonment. When I graduated in 1963, I still did not know what I would be doing, but I did know that I needed to rely on a Guiding Presence. I had now returned to my childhood faith, altered by experience. The power of prayer is not a trite saying nor are the blessings that come from it a "coincidence". Catherine McAuley believed in "constant fervent prayer" (Sullivan, *Correspondence* 93) and because of it, was able to accomplish the unimaginable.

Prayer led me to the unimaginable. After graduating from college, I decided to go to Europe with my best friend. I had always been overprotected so this was a very big step for me. My family was against it, and to entice me, offered to buy me a baby grand piano or to put the money into a savings account. I, unhesitatingly, decided to use this money for my excursion to Europe. My father, literally, disowned me; my mother eventually accepted my decision. So, it came to pass that my girlfriend and I ventured out into the great big world of the unknown. The world we witnessed in our travels was both good and bad. There is something to naiveté and innocence that can engender kindness or cruelty from strangers. We experienced both. After traveling for several weeks throughout Europe, we came to Munich where my cousin was able to find me a job as a monitor/counselor for college girls at McGraw Caserne. It was a one-year commitment which enabled me to stay in Europe. That year became a clincher for who I thought I was. Away from family and friends, I did a lot of soul searching. I fluctuated between who I was before college, during college, and in the current milieu. My identity took a beating in attempting to merge the past with the present. Those were painful times, sprinkled with many tears, but looking back, they were a necessary evolution to a stronger spirituality. What helped to cement my religious beliefs more was my trip to Rome in 1964. There I got a chance to see the Pope and have an audience with Cardinal Joseph Slipyj, family on my father's side. Everything I had read about him defied a simple definition of "heroic martyrdom". My own spiritual battles were miniscule when placed beside a tower of unwavering faith. Cardinal Slipyj had been inhumanely tortured by the communists for his faith. Imprisoned and sent to Siberian hard labor camps, he held steadfastly to his beliefs. He miraculously survived and through the intercession of Pope John XXIII and President John F. Kennedy, he arrived in Rome in 1963 after almost 20 years of animalistic torture. In my brief audience with him, I was awestruck by his presence and manner. His time-worn stature yet keen eyes, coupled with a saintly aura, became a beacon of hope that lessened the turbulence within me about my own faith. Even to this day, his life and trials are a guiding symbol for me. (I was fortunate enough to see him again in 1976 when he toured the U.S. Being family, he did us the great honor of visiting our home in Minneapolis. He was a formidable but very humble figure, his behavior exemplifying a servant approach towards others). Concrete examples of unshaken faith under unbearable torture became an exemplary testament for me of what it means to adhere to and practice Christian love. Later in my teaching career, I found a female counterpart of Christian love - Catherine McAuley - for whom "Jesus was a model, a way to be, a way to live" (Regan and Keiss 45). Both welcomed the cross of Jesus and followed it faithfully. Both followed the advice once given to Catherine McAuley by Edward Armstrong, her close friend: "Do not place your confidence in any human being, but place your confidence in God alone" (Sullivan, *Catherine McAuley* 40).

During that year in Munich as a monitor/counselor, I began to sort out the values that I believed to be my identity. This job gave me experience in handling emotionally wrought young ladies as if I were in control of my own life. In them, I witnessed some of my own struggles (being only two years older than they) and learned through self discipline the practice of compassion. When I was ministering to their needs, I was totally immersed in their lives; however, each human psyche, within quiet reflective moments, has to deal with his/her own inner turmoil - so it was with me. I had many friends, acquaintances, and to the superficial eye, I looked content with who I was. Just as emotions come to a boil because they do not match logic, my striving for interior balance reached its own boiling point. I was beginning to wonder if anyone could ever understand what turbulence I was trying to balance. Only God knew the truth. When I was at my lowest self doubt, I met a young man. He was visiting his family in Munich during Christmas. Through acquaintances he came to our Christmas party.

Being shy and highly introverted, I spoke only with people I knew. He made his way over to my cousin and asked if he could meet me and a conversation evolved which lasted several hours. Later that night I was to write in my journal that I knew there would be a lasting connection between this person and me. The unbelievable had happened. Bohdan actually understood my ramblings about life, religion.

I was right about my intuitive connection with him. This connection is now 45 years old. During my getting-to-know-him time, I found out that he was a student at Louvain on a scholarship, majoring in international relations and previous to that, an ex-seminarian from Rome. This young man had vast knowledge, especially, in theology. I began to be guided by his friendship, love, and deep wisdom. He was making the pieces of the purpose of existence fit within my frantic search for answers. There is a similarity here to Catherine's reliance on the clergy for guidance, especially, her "priest-friend", Edward Armstrong (Sullivan, *Correspondence* 26). Just as I could always rely on my husband's unselfish counsel in anchoring me more strongly in my faith, so did Catherine rely on Edward Armstrong to guide her in spiritual matters. He, himself, attests to their friendship in his will written to Dr. Daniel Murray: "When I shall be taken from her, she will find herself in a great measure bereft of an Ecclesiastical Friend, which is a desideratum for her of the utmost importance" (Sullivan, *Correspondence* 40). My initial attraction to the friendship with my husband was his ability to put a solid frame around my doubts. And although I wasn't building a House of Mercy like Catherine, I was building a secure foundation, block by block, that would eventually allow me to minister to others.

Before I had left for Europe, I had promised my parents I would stay no longer than a year. It was time to keep that promise. However, before I left for Minneapolis, Bohdan and I got engaged, not really knowing how all this would work out. At this point in time, he took it upon himself to write a letter to my parents, explaining how we met and what our intentions were at this point. He also asked for their permission to marry me. They granted that permission with the stipulation that he would need to come to the States. He left his family, his scholarship, his friends, arriving in Minneapolis to a completely foreign environment. We lived with my parents for one year before getting married. During this time, he enrolled at the University of Minnesota although he barely knew any English. He eventually graduated with distinction and a PhD from the University. It was in the later years of our marriage that I asked him what made him persevere in this relationship when he had to make so many personal sacrifices. He simply stated that he was drawn in by the complexity of who I was - like solving an enigmatic puzzle of life. I personally feel that God knew; God acted. He provided us with choices. We listened; we made the right ones. Again, the skeptics may claim coincidences - coincidences where fate brought us together? Highly unlikely. Here are the facts: I left the U.S. where marriage possibilities were not lacking, went overseas, and found a young man who became my husband - not too unusual in itself until one considers that he was also Ukrainian and had been born in the Ukraine only 20 miles away from my birth home. On our wedding day, relatives in the Ukraine from both sides celebrated our wedding. Additionally, through his connections, we received a Vatican document, endorsed by the Pope blessing our union. For me, it all fell together with God as our matchmaker. Thus, we began our marital journey.

Within that journey, the unimaginable became extremely evident as I looked for a career to support my family. With a small child and a husband still in school, I would be the breadwinner for a while. Armed with my B.A. in English and praying fervently, I landed a job as an editorial assistant for a professional magazine. Although I was moving up quickly in my job, I felt restless and dissatisfied. Interaction only with paper left me yearning for some type of compassionate action with others. Within me had always been a burning desire to work with orphans, and this job was far removed from my idealism. The seed within me to work with orphans sprouted during my troubled childhood where separation from the known to the unknown became a way of life, the war years creating a displaced person. DP was a label that became derogatory even in the U.S. especially during my grade school years. Thereby, my early years of life left me powerless in maintaining permanent attachments because I had a registered sense of impermanency within me. These years had created an orphanhood within me even though I had parents. The experience of myriad fearful moments even led to the abandonment of self. However, what life teaches when used in the framework of religion can heighten one's spirituality. I believe a super sensitive awareness arose within me towards the powerless and helpless, especially, the young. While reading Catherine McAuley's life, I was with her emotionally, specifically when she took in an abandoned orphan that had been "cast into the street from a cellar" and "procured conditional Baptism" for the child. "…[H]enceforward the protection of orphans was added to the plan of this institution [Sisters of Mercy]" (Sullivan, *Catherine McAuley* 46). Her sensitivity towards the poor and underprivileged gave shape to her charism of mercy, her love for others.

Being an editorial assistant where paperwork became the predominant occupation of 40 hours of my weekly life intensified my longing to reach out to people other than my family. Worn out by the demands of an unfulfilling job and growing family, on a whim, I decided to look at the want ads not really expecting it to be more than just a temporary diversion. My heart skipped when I read that a Catholic school needed a junior high teacher in English. As my excitement grew about "just trying it", I cast reality aside. Thoughts swirled about not ever wanting to be a teacher, not having qualifying educational coursework, and, horrors, not ever having taught in a classroom. Even if it were folly to apply, something within me pressed me to "just try". With all factual odds against me, I knew that only a miracle could make it a reality. Here I'm reminded of Catherine McAuley's supposed "Kitty's Folly" (Burns and Carney 22) when she faced all odds in building the Baggot Street House. She left the miracle to God and what a miracle it was, the first stepping stone to founding the order and reaching an unimaginable spiritual magnitude throughout the world. Since my decision seemed to be an absurd, spur-of-the-moment one, I prayed for guidance and then zombie-like, applied for the job. When I was granted an interview and immediately hired, I had no time to process the answer, Yes. I was also informed that school would officially start in two weeks. With a smile now, I remember that I was asked to teach "transformational grammar", a new mathematical approach to language. What in the name of heavens was that? With doubt and trepidation, I embarked on a teaching career that, to my amazement, would last for 33 years. In trying to run away from editorial work, I accidentally ran into a teaching ministry which would wind in many directions before I could accept it as a calling.

Ten years were spent in junior high, in three different schools. I had developed a pattern of wanting to change careers every 3 years because I was still convinced I was being called to a different ministry. My initial 3 years were preparatory ones, during which I established a reputation as a good teacher. By word of mouth, I was asked to join the staff of a more renowned school in the area. I did. It seemed that my will was not my own because without hesitation, I would intuitively know that it was the right decision. I think I "let go, let God" without even realizing it. When we moved to Lafayette, Indiana because of my husband's job at Purdue University, I thought my teaching excursions would come to a halt. Not so, Providence had a different plan for me. When we were looking for housing while getting ready for Lafayette, I insisted on renting somewhere close to a church. We were able to secure some housing close to the church and school that my third grader would be attending. I made it a habit to walk him to and from school everyday. One day, I got into a conversation with one of the administrators and found out they were short on subs. I decided I would put my name in. It would give me something to do while I searched for a job.

I subbed for that first school year. When a position in junior high in English opened up the following year, I was invited to apply. Unfortunately, I had to notify them that I was not certified - the strongest requirement for that job. Even though that minimized my chances tremendously, I was given an interview with the parish priest and the school principal. After the interview, they agreed to consider my application if I provided several recommendations from my two previous schools. I still thought it was not doable because I had not taken any education courses; I had envisioned my migratory floatation in education as only a temporary arrangement. The unbelievable happened again - I was hired. It is interesting how shortsighted a human being can be; and even more fascinating, how one can pray to continue that shortsightedness, overriding the omniscience of an ever present God. Even Catherine, in a mild form, experienced an adherence to what she had originally planned which was a desire to form a lay community that would minister to the needy. She battled within herself to avoid forming a religious order, as her letter to Rev. Francis L'Estrange indicates: "…[The] institution in Baggot Street is to go on according to the original intention" (Sullivan, *Correspondence* 41). However, in the larger scope of God's providence, we see her acquiescence to the will of God: "Gradually, Catherine began to understand the importance of ecclesial approval for the stabilization of her work on behalf of poor persons" (Burns and Carney, 25). When I was offered the job in Lafayette because of outstanding recommendations, I began to gradually see that maybe I had a gift that I was stubbornly overlooking - just maybe.

My faith, obviously, was not as stalwart as Catherine's. I still had a lot of short sightedness and misguidance within myself to overcome before I could even begin to understand and appreciate ministry as a teacher. When we moved to New Albany in southern Indiana because of my husband's job, I had immediately become convinced that I was finally in agreement with God's providence. The only agreement, however, that I was in, was with my own wishes. Not having the qualifications needed for teaching nor recommendations that would follow me after a six-year hiatus of non employment to have a second baby, I was sure that the field of education would no longer loom over me. As economic concerns became a factor, I again looked for work. The jobs I seemed interested in required previous experience - a roadblock . After some exhaustive searches in the area, my husband convinced me to go back to school and to stick with being an educator. It looked like the only avenue open to me. However, I would need to get certification. The certification looked problematic because I had officially been out of school for approximately 20 years. Yet "Nothing is impossible with God," as the biblical saying goes. The impossible happened. It was unexplainable in human terms, because at first, I could not even get into the undergraduate program, much less the graduate one. That it was a gift from God became evident to me, especially when a Sister of Charity, who had faith in my abilities, made it possible for me to enter an MAT program at Spalding University. It was a pilot program and I was its first participant. A lot of my coursework was handled through directed reading. I was able to complete this program in a year and a half, receiving a certificate for high academic standing and educational leadership.

Armed with a masters in teaching, I was required to complete a student teaching program at Presentation Academy, although I had already taught for ten years. Here, I can't help thinking of Catherine entering the Presentation novitiate and becoming a professed religious at age 53

(Burns and Carney 25). It was a very humbling experience for Catherine because although she was already a successful foundress she had to be a postulant. Mary Clare Moore, in her account of the experience that Catherine faced at 52, says "It was a severe trial to our Foundress….She also felt difficulty in submitting to the usual restraints and trials of Conventual life…but she offered herself cheerfully to God, to do and suffer all He should appoint in order to accomplish the great work which she felt He had marked out for her" (Sullivan, *Catherine McAuley* 105). In a somewhat parallel way, I knew that my MAT opportunity was a gift from God but I did not have the faith or commitment that Catherine had. I was much more worldly. I was grateful for an opportunity to go back to school and to have a better chance at getting a job.

After completing my student teaching at Presentation Academy, I felt the first flicker of excitement in teaching high school girls. Some of these young ladies were rough and tough, and I found myself challenged by this roughness but loving them more, because that is what I found they needed – an acceptance of who they were. I built a strong rapport with these young girls. I could finally open up as a person. Perfection in my personality did not seem to be so binding. I could laugh at myself with them when, as fortune would have it, I committed a fashion faux pas. In acting out some Shakespearean lines, out of the corner of my eye, I noticed something peeking out from under my slacks around my ankles. Distracted, I pulled at the offender and to my chagrin, found that I had pulled out some bunched up pantyhose that static had imprisoned. A moment of triumph occurred. I had everyone's attention and then a sharing of communal laughter. For the first time in my teaching career, I wanted to stay at Presentation and believed that to be my calling. However, they had no opening, as of yet, for that year. Since I had to pay back my educational loan, I needed to search for a job. I prayed that I would find a suitable one rather quickly. The answer I received within my heart was that besides Presentation, I should apply elsewhere, and the first position offered should be the one I accept. Making this decision, I smugly decided that a position at Presentation would be the first one offered to me. Furthermore, I had not yet taken the teacher qualifying exam for certification so that bought me some time for the opening of my dream at Presentation.

Coincidence or Providence? It so happened that the principals of all Catholic high schools had a meeting. Presentation's principal spoke to Assumption's principal who was looking for an English teacher at the time. I was recommended and before I even realized it, I was on my way to an interview. Of course, I was not duly concerned, because I was sure that Presentation was to be my teaching home. After a somewhat lengthy interview, I was offered a job right on the spot. Trying to control Providence, I lamely stated that I had not yet taken the certification exams for teacher proficiency and asked what would happen if I didn't pass them. I remember the principal's smile as she said, "We'll deal with that when we get there. The job is yours if you want it."

Overwhelmed, I asked if I could wait until tomorrow to give a final answer. I was sure Presentation would call me that night. "No problem," was the answer.

It was no problem for God's Providence. I said yes to Assumption High School in Louisville, Kentucky. However, in the back of my mind, it was temporary employment because I was convinced that I would end up teaching at Presentation soon. Thus at age 43, my 23 years began at this Mercy school where the life of Catherine McAuley was celebrated daily. I had never heard of Catherine but gradually became acquainted with her mission. It took me a long time to realize that the moment I said yes to Assumption, Catherine would be my invisible mentor. She would start me on a journey that would take me emotionally and intellectually to places within me that I had never dreamed existed. I discovered a vast world of possibilities within me, brought about by experiences of joys and sorrows. Prayer during this time became not just a spiritual comfort food, it became an active way of life. It took on a semblance of what Catherine expected of her followers. Catherine told her companions that "Prayer is a plant, the seed of which is sown in the heart of every Christian, but its growth entirely depends on the care we take to nourish it. If neglected, it will die. If nourished by constant practice, it will blossom and produce fruit in abundance" (Degnan, ed., *Retreat Instructions*, 90). This quote sums up the signposts of my life, the places along the way where I stopped to evaluate the direction of my life, and found living water through prayer. "Living with" Catherine McAuley for 23 years has illuminated my past to a merciful present. In my first eleven years of Mercy experience, I gradually became friends with humility and compassion which led to a stronger identity. The next twelve years became the culmination of an indisputable calling - an extroverted love for the ministry of merciful teaching.

Works Cited

Burns, Helen Marie, RSM and Sheila Carney, RSM. *Praying with Catherine McAuley.* Winona: Saint Mary's Press, 1966.

Degnan, Mary Bertrand, ed. *Retreat Instructions of Mother Mary Catherine McAuley.* Westminster, Maryland: Newman Press, 1952.

New American Bible. Wichita: Fireside Bible Publishers, 1994-1995 ed.

Regan, Joanna, RSM and Isabelle Keiss, RSM. *Tender Courage.* Chicago: Franciscan Herald Press, 1988.

Sullivan, Mary C., RSM. *Catherine McAuley and the Tradition of Mercy.* Notre Dame: University of Notre Dame Press, 1995, 2000.

Sullivan, Mary C., RSM, ed. *The Correspondence of Catherine McAuley, 1818-1841.* Washington: The Catholic University of America Press, 2004.

Part II: Mercy in the Classroom: Birth of Values

Through my 23 years of teaching at a Mercy school, Assumption High School in Louisville, Kentucky, I have come to a better understanding of the essence of humility as a representation of Catherine McAuley's life; it is an acknowledgement of gifts to be used in a servant-like outreach towards others. I believe compassion is a child of humility, producing a natural outgrowth of genuine love. Humility coupled with love shapes a life of Mercy. Jesus was the exemplar of Mercy. Regan and Keiss say "…that God , responding to the brokenness or imbalance of humankind, sent his Son to teach us how to be human, to show us the way" (45). Furthermore, Regan and Keiss bring out an essential thought in Jesus' injunction to "…Heal the sick, the lame, the blind. What I want is mercy, not sacrifice" (45). I was especially struck by the last statement "What I want is mercy, not sacrifice". For me it indicates a fine line between intention and behavior in performing acts of mercy. I always felt that if I had compassion, I would be moved to performing acts of mercy. I never questioned the motivation. Now, I see that when the doer considers mercy as a sacrificial act, the good that it was intended to produce becomes a selfish gain. True compassion, I believe, happens when a person is able to forget about the comfort of self and become immersed in the act of doing as a servant. Catherine's journey of mercy was, and is truly authentic and inspirational; she devoted her life to following Jesus' precepts of mercy and love. Burns and Carney point out that "[Catherine] had no great design, only a desire to make some lasting effort for God's poor" (33). Catherine's original intentions were three-fold, even before she established a religious order. In general, she wished to provide an "...education to poor and wretched Girls who could not otherwise procure or obtain it." Secondly, to "...bring together and lodge poor Servant-girls...." And finally, to "...visit the Hospitals and there serve and assist the sick..." (Sullivan, ed., *Correspondence* 43).

She felt that the education of women was of primary importance. In the Rule and Constitutions of the Religious Sisters of Mercy, Catherine very specifically states her reason for this emphasis:

> 5th The Sisters shall feel convinced that no work of charity can be more productive of good society, or more conducive to the happiness of the poor than the careful instruction of women, since whatever be the station they are destined to fill, their example and advice will always possess influence, and where ever a religious woman presides, peace and good order are generally to be found. (Sullivan, *Catherine McAuley* 297)

Thus, as one sees in Catherine's words, the ministry of teaching is a priority and can not be taken lightly. The formation of young minds can be highly influenced by their role models – their teachers. A teacher who believes in God's guidance can hope, with God's help, to instill in students a lasting set of values to live by. Therefore, the teaching ministry with Mercy values at its center may establish a more secure base for future generations.

However, at the outset of my Mercy teaching ministry, I basically fought it as a calling. I was unable to recognize it as a gift. It stood unopened for a very long time, patiently waiting for me to reach a more mature plateau. What is truly ironic is that while negating my calling, I was actually following it. What interests me is how the present constantly beckons us not to put off the gift of now, in preference to the past or the future. Yet somehow, we fail to realize that the past is part of the present, and the future is a created present. Jesus was the greatest teacher who ever lived, performing His acts of Mercy in the daily present. He could have chosen any profession yet his constant pre-occupation was with teaching – with imparting knowledge. According to Regan and Keiss, Catherine and her companions felt this same calling of wanting to instruct the ignorant: "The ignorant they desired to instruct were those whose need was knowledge both to live life productively and to experience the mysteries, the wonders of mind and spirit which contribute to a person's understanding of self and of God" (47). To persistently lead me to follow in His path shows God's compassionate patience with me. I have to admit that it was a while into my teaching ministry before I was able to recognize the altruistic goal set by Catherine McAuley. I could have missed my calling by dwelling on the past.

My path to humility and compassion was in an incipient stage when I started teaching at Assumption. These two qualities were not visibly recognizable in the first part of my Mercy experience. On the outside, it might appear that I had these two values, but they were not internalized enough to approximate the Mercy mission. Yes, I had what looked like humility but it was only its semblance constructed from a doubtful self-esteem; compassion, on the other hand, although implanted in my inner core, was frozen by a fear of rejection. Thus, I would struggle, but learn and develop, in my first eleven years of teaching. I was still waiting for that call to teach at Presentation Academy. It never came. Every so often, I would think about searching elsewhere. In retrospect, I see God's hand in my decision to stay at Assumption.

My first year was one of the hardest at Assumption. In the middle of the year, I became so exhausted that I thought I would not be able to finish the year and was sure that in the eyes of my students, I had failed them. But to my utter surprise, at the end of that year, the student body chose me to get the Jubilee Cup. It is given to a teacher who works behind the scenes for the benefit of the students. They were seeing something in me that I was not yet aware of. Every time I would be plagued with thoughts of inadequacy, I would just look at the cup and know that I should stay. My students needed me. However, it took a long time of positive feedback before I was able to convince myself thoroughly that I was needed here in order to mature correspondingly with my students. I am reminded of the biblical doubting Thomas except that I seemed to be more stuck in my stubborn blindness than he.

Periodically, when my spirits would fail as to whether I was really doing what God wanted of me, I would pray for some type of sign. My human frailty seemed to require many signs. It was almost a bargaining with God, a "show me" plea. This request did not come from arrogance but from a sincere desperation to be on the right path. Whether it would be considered a "coincidence" or not by others, I always was able to recognize internally a sign of hope, a "go ahead" light. Whether it would be a timely retreat note from a student, or a smile from someone smileless, their interjected act would be a signal that I was on the right track. The incident that I remember most, the one that jarred me from myself, happened at the end of a very difficult teaching year. It was the last day of school, and I convinced myself that this would be my last teaching day at Assumption. As I stood in the doorway of my classroom looking at the empty hallways, pondering my possible exodus, a student came up to me. She was not someone I knew. She asked me if I was Mrs. Bochan. I nodded. She handed me an undistinguished but creatively wrapped box and said, "I found this in the bathroom with your name on it." I thanked her and she quickly left. I opened the box slowly without any expectations. Inside was a beautiful gold pin shaped like a tiger. I quickly looked for the giver's name. Inside, a little piece of paper simply stated, "No strings attached. Thank you for everything." There was no name. Although I tried, I was never able to find out who the gift-giver was. I treasure this gift as a symbol of hope. To me it signified that I had "tigrish" strengths and someone just wanted to make me aware of them. I still have the pin and have worn it when I needed confidence. Already my students were teaching me true mercy and humility - the giver was anonymously compassionate.

Slowly, through the eyes of my students, I was beginning to understand that I needed to stop blinding myself and acknowledge the present. In retrospect, I was trying to maintain the image of self that had been crippled by the war years and my cultural upbringing. Growing up, it had been instilled into me that women need not have a developed intelligence. They needed only to look physically pleasing, have impeccable manners, and some artistic accomplishment (e.g. music, art, etc.). It was a formulaic existence with no room for independence. Therefore, it almost seemed a transgression, a source of guilt, to acknowledge any gifts within me that would lead away from this image. I can easily identify with Jane Austen's view of society in *Pride and Prejudice* where women held an unquestioned secondary place in deference to men. The European ideal that I was infused with required a docile being, satisfied with the status quo.

Interestingly enough, I taught my students to be independent, intelligent beings who were in all respects equal to men. Probably the dichotomy within me pushed me all the harder to make these young women acknowledge their own gifts and use them. I guess I could say that I lived vicariously through them, encouraging them to stand up for themselves, something I had not been taught to do.

Up to this point in time, I was teaching advanced students. When I was asked to add students with learning differences to my teaching load, I at first wavered, but soon realized that they were more the type of students that I originally wanted to teach because I understood differences, rejection. During the four years that I taught them, my compassion grew into love and I devised various creative projects and approaches to reinforce their learning style. I invented theories, strategies, of how best to teach them, published some ideas and presented at various LDA (Learning Differences Association) conferences. I met with a lot of success. I finally decided that I had found my niche in teaching and even went back to pick up some certification courses for special ed. I yearned to devote my life to their needs. Thus, I had it all planned for the future. I was happy that my students were doing very well in skill building, and that we were building a strong rapport. Caught up in my own optimism, I became totally oblivious to any undercurrents that could undermine my focus. When they collided with my reality, a new scenario unfolded.

I could explain in detail what transpired to change this reality but it is past; it will suffice to say that my strategies and ideas were too "innovative" for the set curriculum. Unexpectedly, I was informed that I would no longer be teaching students with learning differences. This is when I learned the true meaning of humility. The administration had made a decision and I would not contest it. Overcoming my initial shock, I decided that I could either not come back the following year or grin and bear it. I decided to apply elsewhere. I did. However, odd circumstances again occurred. I applied for a learning differences position at a boys' school to teach students with learning differences and was told they would contact people for interviews within the next two weeks. Three weeks later, my family left for Europe for six weeks. I had not heard from the school in the allotted time; therefore, I assumed I was out of the running. On our return from visiting family in Europe, I had two voice messages: message 1: please come for an interview on…; message 2: due to no response on your part, the position is now filled. I set aside my conflicting thoughts. It was too late to apply elsewhere. I would suffer the year out.

This was my eleventh year of teaching at Assumption - a crossroad. I would definitely be leaving after this year. I would apply early enough this time. To make the year somewhat bearable, I decided to concentrate on publishing some strategies used in the freshman advanced level class. I was successful in my publishing attempts. This active concentration helped me emotionally and psychologically to put things in perspective. I also re-read the numerous notes I had received from my students and was encouraged by them. These affirmative notes helped me to see that it was the students who gave me purpose and, in particular, students at this Mercy school. God was still walking with me through them, and I needed to acknowledge that, even though the present seemed bleak. I was finally maturing spiritually and realizing that my plans were not God's plans, and if I were to rely on His guidance, I would have to let go of my dream and forgive those who had so abruptly erased it. Here again, I am reminded of the Reverend Edward Armstrong's advice to Catherine McAuley: "Do not place your confidence in any human being, but place your confidence in God alone" (Sullivan, *Catherine McAuley* 158). I was the human being in whom I was placing my confidence at first, but through a painful, disappointing journey, I turned to God and learned outward and inward humility. In turn, I was gifted with the best next 12 years of my teaching ministry.

At the end of my crossroad year, I encountered a totally unexpected gift. Our English chairperson had accepted the principalship at Assumption. She had been the AP teacher. I was offered the opportunity of teaching Advanced Placement (AP) students. At first, I did not want to accept the challenge because I had never taught seniors before and felt that it was an uncomfortable intellectual jump. Then the principal told me that when she had asked her AP students who could best teach AP, they named me. I had previously taught them as freshmen. Again, the students were the ones through whom God was working. I accepted tentatively, stating that if I did not do a good job with them that first year, I would decline the position. I have now taught AP students successfully for 12 years. In looking back, I realize that had I made learning differences my total focus, I would have missed out on teaching these fabulous young women. Although they claim I taught them well and prepared them for life, I have to honestly turn that around and state that they have taught me well and prepared me to give credence to myself. What I imparted to them, I realized, was what I was also trying to teach myself - humility, compassion, and love - Catherine McAuley's values for a meaningful temporal journey.

After two years of AP teaching, another gift was offered. The new English chair accepted the position of assistant principal and I was asked to teach her College Placement (CP) class. I again hesitated because I was already teaching AP seniors and advanced freshmen. However, something within me said yes, so I agreed to do it. Eventually, I ended up teaching only AP and CP seniors. Five years into the teaching of these seniors, I received the Karen Russ Excellence in Teaching Award. Although it was a wonderful honor, my biggest award/ honor was being able to teach these gifted young women. It is even hard to adequately explain the joy of learning, of being daily with these gifted seniors. We would explore and analyze to the point where one student aptly commented: "I now know I have a brain, because it hurts." Having an "insight" or being chosen as a "sample paper" brought out euphoric smiles of accomplishment from my students. The material was highly challenging. What made it workable was the role of the teacher as mediator and the application of universal literary ideas to the students' own life experiences. Literature, per se, became a secondary way of life; however, the lessons we learned from it were primary.

Once I accepted myself as an effective communicator of ideas, another gift came my way. My teaching load was lessened by my principal so that I would be able to help out in Campus Ministry. This new assignment totally rounded out what I could offer to others. It was a spiritual enlightenment, a creative way to give back to the Mercy community. In helping the Campus Minister, I became more involved with the spiritual aspect of my teaching ministry. The liturgies, prayer services, special assemblies I helped plan created a deeper understanding of purpose, especially, when my students became active participants. It was also, during this time, that I was inspired to present a reflection on Catherine McAuley for a faculty retreat. The gist of it begins to identify Catherine's mentoring presence in my own teaching ministry. Here is the essence of that personal reflection for that Retreat in Fall 2003. It briefly encapsulates my beginning journey:

Teacher Retreat, Fall 2003

> Who are we as educators? We are the community of Assumption. When we individually enter through the doors of Assumption, we are making a commitment to become Catherine McAuley's emissaries, instruments of mercy. In her Rule, Catherine McAuley aptly said: "No work of charity can be more productive of good society, or more conducive to the happiness of the poor, than the careful instruction of women" (Sullivan, *Catherine McAuley* 297).

> "The careful instruction of women" is our starting point, our mission, as educators of young women, the girls at Assumption. I read a little book, *Praying*

with Catherine McAuley, before I went abroad this summer. I can safely say that Catherine McAuley was with me in East and West Germany, Italy, and the Ukraine. As she haunted my thoughts, I began to define for myself who I am as a person, why I became a teacher, and how I am to carry out Catherine McAuley's mission of teaching young women. In other words, what is each person's individual's mission here, and how does it contribute to a sense of community?

First of all, we must look inwardly to assess who we are. EE Cummings in "A Poet's Advice" wisely states that "To be nobody-but-yourself in a world which is doing its best night and day, to make you everybody else - means to fight the hardest battle which any human being can fight; and never stop fighting". Today, as we listened to statements of one another about who we think we are, it became evident that each one of us battles with identity and with mission. However, what unites all of us ... is that all of us are striving to share our lives, our knowledge, with those we teach. Our goal is the same although our approach may be different.

Ironically, I began to know who I am through teaching. However, I never planned to be a teacher. In fact in 8th grade (many, many moons ago), I shocked the nuns and the priest when I was asked what I wanted to be when I grew up. I said I wanted to be an actress. With mouths agape, they were horrified that I was choosing such an "unholy career". Eventually, I became a teacher through what I call "God's accident". For approximately 11 years, I was simply an imparter of knowledge. It wasn't until I attended a freshman retreat here that I realized that I had a lot of soul searching to do in relation to my students. On that first retreat, I began to understand, just like the freshmen, what it means to be a real, a whole person. In fact, at the end of that retreat a student came up to me and said, "Mrs. Bochan, I never knew you could be such a real person."

"Becoming real doesn't happen all at once" was said on that freshman retreat. I began to lead a retreat each year, and each year, I began to understand more about each student, her struggle to be somebody, regardless of what was going on in her personal life. The most central lesson I learned about all students was that they were very complex beings, in search of self, while beset with numerous personal problems. When I began to see the whole person, I began to teach the whole person. In teaching the whole person, I became more of a whole person. Thus, as we get to know and accept ourselves, we become better educators.

When I finally graduated to leading senior retreats, through the gentle persuasion of our Campus Minister, those experiences became the catalyst for teaching with love. I was no longer just an imparter of knowledge, I now became a participant in the formation of young, gifted women. And as I became more steeped in the mission of Catherine McAuley, I could understand how prayer and service were primary elements in the sturdy growth of young women. The more spirituality we can nurture within ourselves, the more students can see its value and act on it.

I have always tried to make prayer central to my existence but it was more of a mechanical, self-serving device. In teaching, I have found prayer to be the only instrument that helps, even when all else fails. I pray for my students and with my students in the classroom. Initially, classroom prayer rose spontaneously when I decided we needed to pray for a classmate who was dying of cancer. It increasingly became an effective centerin**g** at the beginning of each class period. Each class has its own created prayer that identifies their bond as students in that classroom. At first, however, I was a little hesitant to pray in the classroom until I witnessed its unifying power. The old adage comes back to me, "Those who pray together, stay together." Prayer can take many forms; it need not necessarily be verbalized. Prayer can also take the form of respect for one another and set a climate of openness, of acceptance. My definition of classroom prayer is this: a creation of positive vibrations that generate an atmosphere of love where learning can evolve naturally because the essence of "self" is respected, not threatened.

I believe a commitment to prayer leads to service of others. Service of others is a love extended beyond the self. However, one caution, a person must love herself/himself humbly before that love can be given to others. This was a hard lesson for me to learn. Being a high introvert and relatively insecure, I tended to overdo the expression of love, making it a disciplined sacrifice which bordered on artificiality. When I began to accept myself more, I began to love genuinely. It is now not unusual to laugh at myself in the classroom, to incorporate my weaknesses and strengths into the teaching material, to hug, to cry without feeling censure for who I am. My students relate to me more because I relate to them on a human, imperfect level. I am able to meet their needs better. In not censuring myself, I do not censure them. Service is love. It is love for another human being, one in our care. It is selfless and all encompassing.

The following analogy may help us to understand service. "Service" became clearer to me when I received a Japanese Rose plant from my mother and traveled with the seedling plant for 14 hours by car to New Albany. I was anxious that it survive the trip and kept glancing at it constantly. Once I brought it home, I placed it in the front window so that it could get the sunshine it needed. I watered it religiously. It survived and grew except that one part of it was bent towards the light. I realized that if I wanted it to grow straight, I would have to change its direction periodically. The plant is like our students. We travel in knowledge with them but we should not forget to love them and dutifully care for them. When they bend too much one way, we need to be aware of this and redirect another part of who they are towards the Sun which represents God's love.

Catherine McAuley's vision of prayer and service is truly our mission here at Assumption. I think if Catherine were in our midst physically today, she would smile with approval at who we are and what we are accomplishing for the benefit of our young women. In spite of all odds and difficulties we may encounter, these young women are our Mercy mission. Even the shady Polonius in *Hamlet* can echo truth when he says: "This above all: to thine own self be true, / And it must follow as the night the day, Thou canst not then be false to any man [or woman]" (1.3).

My personal journey today, composed of the past with a foreshadowing future, is like the growth of the biblical fig tree: First, it gave no fruit: "it was not the time for figs" (Mark 11:13). Then, Jesus equates the withered fig tree with faith and the power of prayer: "Have faith in God….Therefore I tell you, all that you ask for in prayer, believe that you will receive it and it shall be yours" (Mark 12:22-24). This for me signifies the beginnings of a reliance on God's providence through the medium of prayer. Finally, Jesus says, "Learn a lesson from the fig tree. When its branch becomes tender and sprouts leaves, you know that summer is near" (Mark 14:28). This brings me to the present where, upon reflection, I see how my pilgrimage has led me to the ripeness of teaching with mercy and love. My present attitude echoes, I hope, a statement Regan and Keiss made about Catherine's mission of mercy:

> For a long time Catherine McAuley would not have been able to put the word on what she was about as "mercy." She discovered mercy at work in her life, experiencing within her concrete situation, her own need. Reflecting on these experiences, she found a sense of God's abiding presence. (45)

Works Cited

Austen, Jane. *Pride and Prejudice*. New York: Bantam Books, 1981.

Burns, Helen Marie, RSM and Sheila Carney, RSM. *Praying with Catherine McAuley*. Winona: Saint Mary's Press, 196

EE Cummings. "A Poet's Advice". 4 March 2009 http://www.thepositivemind.com/HTML/APoet'sAdvicepoem.html

New American Bible. Wichita: Fireside Bible Publishers, 1994-1995 ed.

Regan, Joanna, RSM and Isabelle Keiss, RSM. *Tender Courage*. Chicago: Franciscan Herald Press, 1988.

Shakespeare, William. *Hamlet*. New York: Washington Square Press, 1955.

Sullivan, Mary C., RSM. *Catherine McAuley and the Tradition of Mercy*. Notre Dame: University of Notre Dame Press, 1995, 2000.

Sullivan, Mary C., RSM, ed. *The Correspondence of Catherine McAuley. 1818-1841*. Washington: The Catholic University of America Press, 2004.

Part III: Mercy in the Classroom: Meeting the Challenge

God's abiding presence helps us to meet the challenge of mercy in the classroom. We need to listen to Catherine McAuley's voice calling us to a readiness "...to be authentic, reverent, merciful human beings" (Sullivan, *Catherine McAuley* 35). Catherine asks us to create a loving bond with our neighbor through prayer and service. When we minister to our human brothers and sisters in the daily present, we can experience a genuine love for their total well being. The ministry of reaching out to others can take many forms.

The teaching ministry, as I now see it, is concretely based on Mercy values. The values I have tried to incorporate in my ministry have been humility and compassion which have led to a love in action. I believe that mercy is the hands of love. Burns and Carney clarify the task of Mercy for us by placing it into a framework set up by Catherine: "Perfection does not consist in performing extraordinary actions, but rather in performing extraordinarily well the ordinary actions of every day" (67). Catherine's commitment to this type of Mercy shows us the feasibility of it. Catherine believed "that those mutually drawn by a love of God to the service of others strive to model the gospel life, bestowing the gift of themselves with cheerful, generous, compassionate service..." (Regan and Keiss 82). In companioning with her, we make her an active, living presence in our lives. In reflecting on my 23 years of teaching at a Mercy school, I recognize her evolving presence in my ministry.

In assessing my teaching style, I came to the conclusion that the structuring of knowledge requires more than just factual information. Of primary importance is to establish a positive ambience where students intuitively feel a spiritual thrust within a knowledge-based curriculum and are able to see that modeled in their teacher's behavior. Footnote 79 of Mary Sullivan's comment on "example more than precept" states that "Catherine often repeated her conviction that people learn more by example than by precept, and that Jesus taught chiefly by example" (*Correspondence* 283).

In line with this way of thinking, I always started class with a prayer, specifically tailored to each class. We also included a few of the students' petitions. This briefly gave us a glimpse of each other's lives and bonded us into experiencing positive, other-oriented prayer. Although this beginning prayer would relate to them, it would also designate a responsibility for others' welfare. For example, "Lord, help me to meet the challenges that I face each day and to be aware of my neighbor's needs" was the daily prayer of my College Placement (CP) students. In addition, if there happened to be a crisis locally or nationally, I would ask them to form a circle and then I or a volunteer would say a few words of spiritual comfort. On a happy note, we also did the circle form for birthdays, singing happy birthday and ending with a group hug. These small prayer occasions set an atmosphere of acceptance, compassion, and love. I found that factual material was retained better because of the minuscule spiritual bonding with which we would set the tone for the whole class.

The beginning of the school year always brought the syllabus to life. On the first day of class while going over the syllabus, I would explain to my students that there was only one rule to adhere to in this class. They always liked this statement; however, they soon realized the impetus of it. The rule was based on only one word - respect - but its ramifications were countless. When they understood the repercussions of this word, they, at first regarded it as an intruder, but eventually, accepted it as a necessary "giant". In processing this concept of respect, I would ask them to think of people they esteem and then, to list the appropriate behavior towards them. Through their own comments, they began to realize that they needed to initiate proper behavior towards others by accepting who they are, and acknowledging their worth as a human being. Furthermore, respect is synonymous with veneration which implies "an almost religious attitude of reverence and love" (*Webster's Dictionary* 1147). I think that Catherine would approve of this extended meaning since "…Catherine and [the] first Sisters of Mercy cherished as the essence of the charism which they had received, the recognition and the fostering of the dignity of every human person" (Regan and Keiss 47). In showing dignity, a person shows less of self-importance and more of other-importance. This necessitates a humbler, more compassionate stance that confirms the worth of others. In my classroom, it becomes a given that I respect the students and they, in turn, respect each other and me. This mutual respect begins to pave the way for solidifying Christian values. When each one in the classroom is reminded to model respect towards one another, a more peaceful, charitable atmosphere emerges and quality learning can take place.

With prayer and respect comes a freeing of one's being, an openness, towards one another and the material to be learned. This attitude of openness reinforces a stronger communal bond. Ingraining a tradition of prayer and acceptance into the classroom fits with Catherine's goal for building her own community: "that all who gathered as [H]is followers were to be united in love for God and for one another" (Regan and Keiss 44-45). The teacher's role in imparting knowledge in this type of milieu fits Catherine's precept "that we may impart such instruction as will lead them to God, and keep ourselves faithful in our duty" (Sullivan, *Correspondence* 460). To be "faithful in our duty" as educators is to give our best in teaching the whole person - every person. Each student needs our individual attention and needs to be reached by our extension of love. In an overburdened classroom, this sometimes does not seem to be a working practicality; however, just noticing body language or extending a simple smile or greeting to the lost one in our class helps strengthen the human connection. Here, I am reminded of a student that I had in homeroom for four years, but never actually taught. Senior year, she thanked me for my, every morning, well-wishing to "have a good day". This was a tough homeroom, and at times It was difficult to sincerely utter those words, but they evidently made a difference. Being kind, generous, and compassionate, even in small things, is Catherine's call to all of us.

I think when I began to concentrate more on the needs of each individual in my classroom, I found myself devising lesson plans that would actively engage each student by capitalizing on individual strengths. Catherine corroborates this view when applying "The Chapter on Union and Charity in the Rule of the Presentation Sisters" to her own order. She " [i]nterpreted this chapter [by giving] focus to [each one's] spirituality, demanding that each respect and reverence another's gifts, talents, and disposition, as well as accept each individual's physical, emotional, psychic, and spiritual limitations. It created unity within variety…" (Regan and Keiss 98). Her all-inclusive words can be applied to our daily teaching ministry of creating daily lessons where even subject matter produces "unity within variety". Recognizing the needs of my students, I constructed innovative strategies to motivate and stabilize the learning process in my classroom. The higher the diversity in my classroom, the more my inventive projects took shape.

When I was introduced to the theory of multiple intelligences at a school in-service session, I realized that it resembled what I originally was trying to accomplish in my classroom but, of course, in a more simplistic way. I would create projects that entailed group work where each individual was given a task according to her talent or interest. Evaluations of these types of projects were comprehensive: written and performance based. The students experienced success when working collaboratively with an invested interest. My ideas became reinforced through consulting Howard Gardner's works on multiple intelligences. He firmly advocated that the scope of a student's ability should not be limited to only one stereotypic measure which, for me, made educational sense. In the "Epilogue" of his book *Multiple Intelligences*, he comments that he "[hopes] that the idea of multiple intelligences will become part of teacher training" (251). Furthermore, he states that "should a sensitivity to different intelligences or learning styles become part of the 'mental models' constructed by new teachers, the next generation of instructors are far more likely to be able to reach each of their students in the most direct and effective way" (251). When students begin to take pride in their work, they are more cooperative and more likely to accept themselves and others, thus, exhibiting a more positive behavior. Therefore, it becomes important to research various methods so that the most effective strategies can be utilized. Catherine McAuley in planning to meet the needs of her future students also "studied teaching methods" (Regan and Keiss 23) because she believed that "long-term improvement of the condition of the poor depended on education of the young…" (23). I think her words can be universalized by considering among "the poor" all those who are bereft of necessary knowledge for whatever reason. Unless we make a concerted, conscious effort to help our students reach their potential in wholesomeness, we can fall short in our Mercy ministry.

I found that a measured IQ did not adequately recognize each student's pending ability nor spiritual potential. Besides building on the idea of multiple intelligences, I became aware that I needed an overall strategy that could meet the needs of the verbally challenged students in my learning-differences classes. I knew from my teaching experiences so far, that the answer to student success lay in the strategies used in the classroom and in the established classroom atmosphere: two elements that definitely fostered growth in knowledge and character formation. In teaching both advanced freshmen and learning-differences students, I soon discovered that the inherent ability to learn a complex concept was equal in both groups. The learning-differences students could master the same complex material as the advanced ones if I could pinpoint their weakness and work around it. Experimenting with various ideas, I constructed what I termed an "imagistic theory". This theory when put into practice helped to eliminate an incongruity that often existed between a student's thinking process and his/her ability to translate thought into standard language. To assist the verbally challenged students, I devised projects centered on one major factor: the use of concrete images that eventually became translated into language form. When I applied this theory to classroom use, I saw that students were empowered by it. When students are challenged, but can successfully overcome this challenge, they become more confident. Paying meticulous attention to the needs of students, spurs us on to tailoring material that can become "student friendly". Even more crucial for these students with a distinct learning style, or really for any students, is to construct a secure, loving environment, one of "unconditional patience" if we want them to be able to thrive in the classroom, not only intellectually but also emotionally and spiritually. Just as "Catherine and her associates prepared unlettered and untrained young women with skills which enabled them to value themselves and to be valued in turn" (Regan and Keiss 28), so should we, as educators of youth, equip them with living skills that generate a meaningful direction. Furthermore, Catherine advises that "The employments which regard our neighbor require that we should be very well grounded in humility and patience – in order to be truly serviceable to them without any prejudice to ourselves" (Sullivan, *Correspondence* 459).

Throughout my first eleven years at Assumption, I took in only bits and pieces of who this person, Catherine McAuley, was. I was impressed with the factual information about her life, but her unique view of charism was still out of my reach. Although I loved my students, I simply taught with a creative bent, concentrating mostly on externals. Catherine's living presence did not become evident to me until my last twelve years of teaching. As Catherine became my steadfast friend, my intuitive motivator, I found myself more immersed in her value system, and more propelled by the Mercy charism. "Catherine McAuley is remarkable for the manner in which she embodied the ordinary virtues in her daily life" (Burns and Carney 14). I became more "ordinary" that is, natural, in my way of teaching. I changed my approach from a giver of knowledge to a total participant. It was during the time that I taught the AP (Advanced Placement) and CP (College Placement) students that I indubitably felt her presence. It influenced me to look at learning as a reciprocal process. I eased into the position of moderator, opening the knowledge base to my students and only interjecting as needed to clarify or enrich a point under discussion. When I adapted the principles of the Socratic Seminar to my students' needs, their literary discussions scintillated with literary insights which they then made applicable to the universal values of their own lives. Although acquisition of knowledge is necessary, I realized that it was not an end in itself but a vehicle for understanding the mechanism of selfhood.

To illustrate the Socratic procedure, I will provide an excerpt from the type of questions that I would formulate to bring out both factual knowledge and personal values. This particular seminar was based on *Oedipus the King* by Sophocles. The general directions for this seminar were as follows: To apply the question first to the actual play, quoting directly, and then, to self and world:

1. When is free will truly free or are we simply governed by fate?

2. How can self-knowledge be painful? Beneficial?

3. How can Oedipus be/not be a role model for us?

4. Construct your own meaningful question that can be based on Oedipus and is debatable.

I found the Socratic Seminar format to be an ideal tool for value enrichment. Of course, the humanities lend themselves more to this type of critical thinking exercise, but I would envision that math, science or any other subject could follow the same prototype to achieve knowledge of subject and of self. The Socratic Seminar provides open opportunities for students to explore concepts within the value system of their own world. The teacher moderator facilitates the discussion with in-depth questioning, encouraging a formation of positive outcomes. In this type of framework, knowledge is generated and sifted through student minds rather than through teacher power. Student ownership of ideas becomes firmly established. Keeping abreast of strategies that work for our students is of primary importance to their total development.

An even more ideal situation is infusing the total curriculum with a set of values that are incorporated into the specific subject matter. I was fortunate to be allowed to create a one-year thematic curriculum for my CP students which worked very well. Here is a brief outline of this thematic approach: The year's work in CP English was titled: "An Epiphany: Search for

Identity". It was composed of four units with comparable literary works suited to the stated theme of each unit. Exploration of ideas was both intellectual and self applicable.

Unit I: Fate vs. Free Will; **Unit II**: Appearance/Illusion; **Unit III**: Reality; **Unit IV:** Mission of Identity. Each unit explored two literary works that lent themselves to the theme specified. Each unit's theme complemented each other, cumulatively merging into a search for identity, not only literary, but also, personal.

Unit III, based on facing reality, is a good example of a synthesis of literary knowledge with an acquisition of values, focusing on self understanding and compassion. This unit's final product was a research paper based on either the novel *Night* by Elie Wiesel, dealing with the Holocaust or *One Day in the Life of Ivan Denisovich* by Alexander Solzhenitsyn, dealing with Siberian labor camps. In addition to a novel, they were also required to research human atrocities in the 20th century. Under the umbrella of "man's inhumanity to man", they analyzed the selected literary work in relation to a recorded inhumane event from the 20th century. Each student chose a different event to pursue. When all the class work was completed, the students were exposed to a vast historical array of inhumane behavior. The knowledge base and understanding of human behavior they acquired was comprehensively mind boggling. They became saturated with factual information laden with a core of human values.

The first lesson that they learned through this project was that "man's inhumanity" did not start nor end with the Holocaust or the labor camps. Initially, they are horrified that the world stayed silent, allowing such torture and mass graves. Then, slowly there is an awakening that atrocities have not stopped and are even happening in today's world. Although they show some compassion for and disbelief of the cruelty that one human being can inflict on another, they still feel exonerated because they were neither perpetrators nor participants in these inhumane events. However, an epiphany occurs when some of their daily behavior is scrutinized, indicating a lack of sensitivity towards others, to the point of discrimination.

Through analyzing and synthesizing factual information, they become intellectually well informed. But before they can write their research paper, we hold various types of Socratic discussions that delve into moral issues. The most poignant lesson learned through this process is that all of us are at times guilty of "inhumanity to man and woman", maybe not on a grand world scale, but on a microcosmic one. Everything can start with a small action that can metamorphose into macrocosmic proportions. For example, a selective choice of friends that excludes others on the basis of some insignificant criteria such as wealth, fashion, looks, etc. can be classified as discrimination. Isn't that what happened in the Holocaust where discrimination took millions of lives? The students soon begin to see reality when they pit their action against a larger tapestry of humanity; they attain an ability to identify how each negative perception can ease into becoming a silencer of true values. The most astounding realization for them is that they too can be guilty of "man's inhumanity" on their own level. Prejudicial judging of others without first examining oneself can be likened to the passage in the Bible where Jesus says

"…remove the wooden beam from your eye first; then you will see clearly to remove the splinter from your brother's eye" (Matthew 7:5). The main lesson learned here is that each one of us through self examination can become a potent force for eradicating hatred. Finding honesty in oneself and maintaining it can help each one of us generate a positive impact on our world. And just as negativism can grow through small acts, so can a positive attitude. This positive attitude implies the building blocks of faith, hope, and love. The Bible reinforces this human commitment to honoring one's neighbor: "So faith, hope, love remain, these three; but the greatest of these is love" (Corinthians 1:13). Love is the epitome of acting with mercy. It brings hope and increases faith.

Although my AP (Advanced Placement) curriculum was also thematically based, its structure was more manifold and rigorous since part of the emphasis was the standardized test at the end of the year. Thematically, we dealt with social and historical values. Every novel, drama, poem was referenced against a general background of these values. In Socratic Seminars, class discussions, critical essays on these works, students were encouraged to dialogue about values portrayed in the works and compare them to today's views. Although many themes arose from these works, students were channeled to concentrate on heroism, or lack of it, fate, love, power and independence. Love and independence led the list for initiating positive character formation. In this class, I concentrated heavily on community building to emphasize a mutual reliance on one another. What I instituted at the beginning of the year was to have each student choose from a general genus a particular species that most resembled them personally. Every succeeding year, each AP class was given a new genus to select from. For example, one category was insects. Throughout the year, we would create metaphors or humorous statements regarding our insect. Of course, we composed our daily prayer that implied our flight towards wisdom and the needs of our neighbor. By the end of the year, we would create such a strong bond that indeed Shakespeare's words "Parting is such sweet sorrow" (*Romeo and Juliet* 2.2) could have become the AP motto.

An illustration of our closeness by the end of the year was evidenced through either written or given goodbye speeches. Of course, as a teacher I also participated. Here is one example of the yearly goodbye I wrote to an AP class that intimates the bonding that occurred.

THE BUTTERFLY BLINK

(We were all different kinds of butterflies that year.)

Definition: If you blink your eye, it is like a wave of a butterfly wing, simultaneously saying hello and goodbye –from Bochan's personal dictionary.

Since you are the hardest class to say goodbye to, I have devised the paradoxical butterfly blink that merges goodbye with hello, equaling goodello or simply, a wet eye blink.

For most of you, cocooning started as early as freshman year. Then came senior year and you were asked to come out of your cocoons. Each one of you struggled, in your own way, to break the bonds of cocoonism as insight threatened your existence. As you emerged, your colors were always radiant; however, your flight seemed just a little "erratic".

It became evident towards the end of the year that you could get your wings into a parallel position (like a thesis), strengthen the body (organization) and fill the air with color and beauty (insight). The awesome aspect of your flight became your ability to either fly solo or in swarms (peer revisions), achieving a meaningful, original journey (end product).

And Socratic Seminar? Socrates would have taken you on as his own swarm of butterflies, but I would have fought him for it since I always have the last word (according to my family), and I would have won. So much for Socratic wisdom.

On a very sentimental note (butterflies have a heart): I will always treasure the drove of butterflies prayerfully pasted onto the "artifice" on my dining room table. I will always remember your support, emotional and prayerful. It caused many butterfly blinks of gratitude when I was in need of your strength.

Although in the future you may be out of my view physically, you will never disappear from my fond memories, and whenever I happen to have "down flights", I will remember your caring flutter.

I leave you with a promise: When I see butterflies, I will think of you, and when I don't see them, I will still think of you. And when you see white butterflies, know that I am sending you positive thoughts: We have brushed wings and become the better for it.

My butterfly heart wishes you the best life can offer while I blink a "goodello".

Prayers, Peace and Love.

Two more examples provide an even stronger glimpse of AP bonding and spiritual direction. One is a letter to my class of "foliage" and the other is a student letter to her classmates about the AP "foliage" experience. Both of these are included to indicate a spiritual depth of experience that echoes Catherine McAuley's way of life.

Dearest Foliage,

The unity of nature and humankind is the mystery of the cycle of life. Therefore, it is a fact that you are both nature and humankind manifested in your chosen foliage for this year and a beautiful mystery within yourself (syllogism?). The AP garden is the most unique and exquisite one because it contains a myriad of greenery, yet each bit of foliage is individually identifiable. No other garden will ever be like this one: Where will you ever get this unbelievable variety and growth? From grass to trees, to flowers to veggies, we have it all!

The AP foliage has been pruned and nurtured, blossoming into knowledge. Every blade of grass, of flowers, trees, even veggies euphoniously sings a melody of self-knowledge. This melody heard in the microcosm of Room 300 also permeates into the surrounding macrocosm. This spirit of harmony blows through the foliage whispering life's secret: that to be who you are is God's mysterious gift to you, that to become who you will yet be, is to continue to be who you are.

Just as grass cannot be a tree, nor a veggie a flower, so can you not be who you are. The Creator creates only beauty, and you, in your own individuality, are all precious and beautiful. If you ever doubt this fact, go out into nature and notice the perfection of each piece of foliage. Amazing isn't it? How much more awesome are you because you are in God's true image? Believe in the beauty of nature, believe in yourself.

Your knowledge, your giving foliage, has done wonders for me, a mimosa tree. Although I have shared in only a miniscule fraction of your lives, you have created the most meaningful and beautiful blossoms on my mimosa tree. As your foliage grows elsewhere, I will be reminded of your gifts and beauty every time I see mimosa blossoms.

Dear garden, I wish you growth and success, but most of all, I wish you love: love of self and others. Thank you for the privilege of learning from and teaching you. I will have a constant reminder of all of you in the works of nature, from the little fragile flower to the tallest trees, from grass that needs mowing to the veggies in my salad.

And so ends the cyclical four years with a new season of knowledge beckoning your way. Green will again be your color but it will be a richer color, because you have allowed yourselves to be who you are.

God bless you always,

Mimosa Tree

Here is an AP English Farewell Speech by a student to her classmates:

Foliage

Listen. Can you hear that? I think it's raining - soft drizzling rains in some parts, and in other areas, it's pouring. The rain seems unstoppable. But these "mourning" rains are not eternal, my friends. For, after the rain comes the sun. In truth, the sun was there all along - watching from a distance. The sun was always loving, nurturing, and guiding us.

Brrr. Can you feel that? I think it's the wind - swiftly, wildly blowing. I think the winds are changing. Don't worry though, friends, the wind will not tear up your roots - but is rather just taking your seeds away from home, the home they have known to a new and different place - to a new garden.

Our old garden, our garden here, has been beautiful. Do you remember when we were first brought to this garden? Some of us knew exactly where we were, exactly where we wanted to go and planted ourselves right away. Others tried to grow in this soil here and found that it didn't work out, and then tried to grow in that soil over there and found that didn't work out either. Some of us tried to grow on top of a rock or in the stream. Whew! Eventually, however, we found where we needed to go. (Some of us didn't even want to be a plant; we thought we would rather be a duck or a rock.) Finally, we all planted ourselves, took hold of our heritage as plants, and began to…well, we began to sprout.

Remember the first time the Gardener visited us? She had this really big watering can that just scared us to death. She kept saying how we needed more water, more sunlight. I thought I would drown in all that water, or burn because of too much sunlight. She kept telling us to grow and stretch, but I had thought that I already had. I listened anyway, and to my surprise…I grew. After some time, I stopped really paying attention to my own growth and looked around me. Wow! I was truly in a beautiful garden. I had never realized how gorgeous we all were, and how we depended and grew from the help of one another.

What does it take to really make a garden grow? It takes the solid foundation of soil and grass - grass that can speak the language of many different plants, knowing how to nourish them. It takes the quiet strength of the plants that seem to stand independently on their own, for they motivate the other plants to believe in themselves. It takes the organized plants to know what to do now, later, and what to look forward to. It takes the plants that first wanted to be pessimistic and grow towards the ground to find a reason to be optimistic and grow towards the sun. It takes the detailed-oriented plants, whose position towards the sun has been perfected to a mathematical certainty to know exactly at what angle they must stand in order to get the most sunlight. It takes the plants that stretch in every single direction, even directions I'm not sure they're supposed to grow in, to encourage the other plants to stretch and think, too. It takes the loud plants to encourage and motivate others to do their best by cheering on all of the foliage. It also takes dedicated and hardworking plants to share the knowledge they've gained with their friend plants. And it takes the plants that keep us grounded by telling us the direct truth about our state of growth. It also takes a Gardener, someone to water and tend the soil. Someone to love and encourage the plants to be the best they can be. Even a Gardener, on occasion can wear a skirt and jiggle. More than anything, it takes the sun - the eternal light - that guides both the plants and the Gardener.

My friends, we have been planted, we have grown, we have eliminated all stifling boundaries and reached our full potential…in this garden at least. It is time for us to expand our horizons, to let our seeds fly, and to enter a new garden of adventure and opportunity.

But look. Can you see that? Look around you. Look at the colors - the diversity of knowledge and experience in our garden. Look at the varying colors of personality in this room. Look at the *incredible rainbow these colors create. For after the rain, comes the sun. And after this sun, comes the rainbow. We are that rainbow. Stand tall, and show the world the rainbow of love that our garden has created. You are beautiful, you are unique, and you are life and love in its greatest form. Believe in yourselves, and know that our garden will always grow together. I love you all and wish you much growth, happiness, and love.*

Good luck, I know you will all do amazing things! (Jamie Smeland, 2002)

My students brought Catherine McAuley to life for me because they demonstrated her vision through seeing themselves as worthwhile, through reaching out to their classmates, and through practicing compassion towards one another. Being in a Mercy school provided their rich soil, while growth came from their individual experiences within the classroom. My fortuitous teaching ministry under Catherine's spiritual tutelage, manifested through daily interactions with others, has opened my eyes to firmly believe in God's providence and to try sincerely to live out the two commandments of Jesus: "You shall love the Lord your God, with all your heart, with all your soul, and with all your mind. This is the greatest and the first commandment. The second is like it: You shall love your neighbor as yourself" (Matthew 22:38-39). It's a tall order from the Bible, but it gives meaning to life as it should be lived. Catherine McAuley dedicated her life to following it. So although I cannot live it out as well as Catherine, I can at least try to follow her lead. My immersion into the Mercy charism has produced many Catherine McAuley moments. As a matter of fact, the last 12 years of teaching have constituted a marathon run of keeping up with Catherine's charism of giving oneself. It has become a life-long lesson that will not end with my teaching ministry.

Works Cited

Burns, Helen Marie, RSM and Sheila Carney, RSM. *Praying with Catherine McAuley.* Winona: Saint Mary's Press, 1966.

Gardner, Howard. *Multiple Intelligences.* New York: Basic Books, A Division of Harper Collins Publishers, 1993.

Regan, Joanna, RSM and Isabelle Keiss, RSM. *Tender Courage.* Chicago: Franciscan Herald Press, 1988.

Shakespeare, William. *Romeo and Juliet.* (Arden Shakespeare: Second Series). 27 March 2009 <Shakespeare.mit.edu

Solzhenitsyn, Alexander. *One Day in the Life of Ivan Denisovich.* Trans. E.P. Dutton & Co. New York: The New American Library Inc., 1963.

Sophocles. *Oedipus the King.* Trans. Bernard Knox. New York: Washington Square Press Publication of Pocket Books, 1994.

Sullivan, Mary C., RSM. *Catherine McAuley and the Tradition of Mercy.* Notre Dame: University of Notre Dame Press, 1995, 2000.

Sullivan, Mary C., RSM, ed. *The Correspondence of Catherine McAuley, 1818-1841.* Washington: The Catholic University of America Press, 2004.

The New American Bible. Wichita: Fireside Bible Publishers, 1994-1995 ed.

Webster's College Dictionary. New York: Random House, Inc., 1991.

Wiesel, Elie. *Night.* Trans. Marion Wiesel. New York: Hill and Wang, A Division of Farrar, Straus and Giroux, 2006.

Part IV: Living Catherine McAuley Moments

Accepting our ministry in life can be likened to that of prayer; meeting our ministry's challenge can be our call to service. In doing both, prayer and service, we begin modeling Catherine McAuley's passion for leading a life of Mercy, thereby, creating Catherine McAuley Moments. As soon as I became aware of her influence in my ministry of teaching, I was able to acknowledge moments of her presence. The more I thought about her gift of charism, the more I realized that I was trying to follow her lead. I now have accumulated 23 years of Catherine McAuley Moments – encounters of spiritual harmony where unexpectedly the giver simultaneously becomes a receiver while ministering to others. The giver's selflessness helps to create a moment where the temporal and eternal briefly fuse into an epiphanic realization which, for me, can be symbolically likened to Michelangelo's painting "The Creation of Adam" where the Creator meets the created through the touch of an extended finger, illuminating the God/man bond of love. A further connective clarification can be found in Portia's words from Shakespeare's *Merchant of Venice:*

> The quality of mercy is not strain'd,
>
> It dropeth as the gentle rain from heaven

Upon the place beneath: it is twice blest;

It blesseth him that gives and him that takes…

It is an attribute to God himself; (4.1)

"It blesseth him that gives and him that takes." Incorporating these words into my own framework of experience, I find the Catherine Moments to be of this same dual potency: selfless giving generates unexpected moments of receiving, intensifying "the quality of [M]ercy".

For me, "giving" has been a conscious effort to minister to others either through knowledge or prayer. Not only in the classroom can a teacher build a value system on a daily basis, but she/he can also find other related opportunities for solidifying value acquisition. For example, although I had already retired from teaching in 2008, I was invited to present a values session dealing with dream interpretation during Assumption High School's Mission Week in February of 2009. When teaching previously at Assumption High School in Louisville on a full-time basis, I had found the girls to be very intrigued by dream interpretation. Therefore, this particular invitation became an opportunity to capitalize on their interest while incorporating Mercy values. I was happy to present a values session that could encourage the girls to view dream interpretation as an aid to creating a stronger set of personal values.

First of all, I introduced dream interpretation as a tool for establishing their own values, emphasizing that it is a gift from God that helps us to better understand ourselves and the world we live in. I informed them that if they recorded their own dreams and spent time thinking about them, they would gain insight into who they are. Furthermore, I made them aware that dreams have a biblical origin in both the Hebrew scriptures and the New Testament. Then, I supplied them with an explanatory handout about dream formation. The theme emphasized in this student handout was the following:

Dream interpretation is about you – the total you. It is the fusion of your outside and inside world. It can put into perspective your individual identity within your realm of reality. If you want to find out who you are, pay attention to your dreams. If you do this often enough, you will find that your understanding of self, relation to God, and the values you hold are clearer and the unknown more known.

In presenting this information, I had their rapt attention because I was adding knowledge to an enigmatic unknown in their lives, showing them how concrete reality metamorphoses into abstract, yet symbolic, configurations that supply answers to their own questions. This is only one small example of how values can be reinforced outside of the regular classroom. Any extra-curricular activities can present myriad ways of identifying values, whether the teacher is modeling them or simply clarifying them for students.

Another area of "giving" slowly arose from my helping out with retreats and other activities of Campus Ministry. On those occasions I was challenged to create "spiritual sproutings" - outreaches - that echoed Catherine's vision of unwavering faith in God's Providence. On one of the earliest freshman retreats I led, I was asked to construct a story that would show outreach, a moving away from self to others. As I re-read it recently, I recognized my fledgling attempt at Catherine's vision of merciful outreach. The Bridge-it story projects my own spiritual enclosure at the time. Bridge-it's search, written 20 years ago for freshmen, encapsulates my own beginning journey.

BRIDGE-IT

There was once a lonely little castle who couldn't understand why she was so lonely. She knew she was created by God, so she must be a beautiful structure, especially on the inside, because the Creator had taken special care that no two structures were alike. She also knew the inside could not be defective because God never makes rejects. She realized that if an inside became defective then it was due to the owner's lack of upkeep. Bridge it was sure, she thought, that she had cultivated all the gifts God had given her. However, she was confused; she could not understand why she was so lonely.

She thought back to her day of creation as far as she could remember, to the days when she was just a baby castle. She tried really hard to remember what she had learned throughout the years. "Somewhere lies the answer to the riddle of my loneliness, but where?" she asked herself.

When one tries really hard to remember something, one goes over and over the same things hoping some clue will appear to solve the mystery. Bridge-it did this. As she concentrated to the best of her castle ability, the following thoughts flowed out:

I love God.

I value myself.

I love and care for my neighbor.

And then, she suddenly stopped and almost screamed into the stillness: "Yes, yes, I do, but does anyone else know this, other than myself? That's it, that's it," she thought. "Bridge-it, Bridge-it, you forgot to bridge-it." She continued in deep thought: "Yes, all of us castles have been made with a drawbridge." Suddenly, she was seized with a horrible thought: "What if it was too late to open the drawbridge? What if no one wanted to share her love? What if they laughed at her because she was different? What if…?" She quickly pushed her doubts aside and let down her drawbridge before she could lose her courage and determination.

Lo and behold, there was a new world out there. A gentle breeze blew in, reviving all her feelings. There was a beautiful world out there that beckoned and challenged her to taste and assist that world. No longer hesitating, Bridge-it knew what direction her life should take. With the drawbridge now wide open, Bridge-it's little lonely voice got carried by the wind with a new force, new energy as it confidently proclaimed to the world: Life is of little value if the treasures stay hidden and eventually rust and deteriorate. One must share with others through openness and receptivity; one must risk exposure if one is to truly live:

In the love of God,

Out of the love of self,

Into the love of our neighbor.

Can you hear a little lonely castle calling? Can you dare to let down your drawbridge and answer its call?

Answering "the castle's call" came much later in my teaching ministry for "When I was a child [spiritually], I used to talk as a child, think as a child, reason as a child" (1Corinthians 13:11). Eventually, more mature "spiritual outreaches" occurred, especially, when I was asked to lead prayer. The prayers I constructed during my years in Campus Ministry began to indicate a deeper recognition of Catherine's presence in my own life. For example, I created "A Dialogue with God" as a morning prayer to help meet the spiritual needs of faculty members.

A Dialogue with God

God is the Potter.

We are the clay.

God's time is not our time.

God's ways are not our ways.

God says, "Let me fashion you

According to My image."

We answer: "Let me first

Meet my earthen goals;

Let me buy eternity."

"But I AM eternity.

Trust me to mold, shape

And enkindle your life."

"Lord, as you mold and shape me,

Let me choose my own path,

For many times, my time

Is not Your time;

My ways are not Your ways."

Ulana M. Bochan

"My own beloved creation,

I have given you free will,

Love and life.

Choose to trust Me to lead you.

For when you choose Me,

Your time is My time,

Your ways are My ways.

Your path becomes eternity.

Amen.

The last stanza personifies Catherine McAuley's life journey – a total commitment to following the footsteps of Jesus. Regan and Keiss emphasize this commitment: "For [Catherine] Jesus was model, a way to be, a way to live" (45).

Another prayer, "Let There Be Light", prays for the help to minister to each other with the gifts we have been given. I composed it for the closing meeting of the Campus Ministry Board. It is an interactive prayer that attempts to give credence to each member's dedication to the Mercy mission: to be a light to each other and the world.

LET THERE BE LIGHT

Leader: When God created the universe,

HE said, "Let there be light."

The light broke through the darkness.

All: LET THERE BE LIGHT

Leader: When God sent Jesus into our world,

He said, "Jesus is the light of the world."

His light will dispel our darkness,

Will create within us

The potential to be

A light in our own world.

All: LET THERE BE LIGHT IN OUR OWN WORLD.

Leader: The flicker of a candle

Is a transporter of hope.

One ray arrayed with many

Lights up the darkest room.

All: LIGHT, A TRANSPORTER OF HOPE, LIGHTS UP THE DARKEST ROOM.

Directions for interaction: Form a circle in preparation for lighting each other's candle in succession. The Leader with a lit candle will light the candle of the person to the left of her/him saying the following:

Leader says, "You are the light in your world; you light up the darkest room.

After the candle is lit, the candle person responds:

"I am a light in our world. I will light up the darkest room with my light of (either faith, hope, or love) by... (name an action, finishing your own thoughts here.)

After everyone has lit a candle and spoken, the room becomes embraced by circular candlelight; the circle is then designated as Part A and Part B for response purposes.

(Half Circle A): LET THERE BE LIGHT

(Half circle B): LET THERE BE LIGHT IN OUR WORLD.

(Half Circle A): WE ARE THE BEARERS OF LIGHT IN OUR OWN WORLD.

(Half Circle B): LIGHT, A TRANSPORTER OF HOPE,

ALL (full circle): LIGHTS UP THE DARKEST ROOM!

Leader: WHERE THERE IS LOVE AND HOPE WITHIN OUR COMMUNITY, THERE IS FAITH THAT THE LIGHT WE BRING TO OTHERS WILL COME FROM OUR GOD OF THE UNIVERSE, AND THE LIGHT OF THE WORLD, JESUS.

ALL: AMEN.

Catherine McAuley was the brightest light of her time, ministering to the poor, forsaken, and uneducated. She is still the brightest illumination of what we, as her emissaries, need to carry out "[in] undertaking the arduous, but very meritorious duty of instructing the poor " (Sullivan, *Catherine McAuley* 295). The "poor", in our modern day view, could be the ones in need of our extension of faith, hope and love. If we minister to those in need, Catherine says, "[w]e may then truly say to [those under] our care what Saint Paul said to the Philippians and Thessalonians: 'You are my joy and my crown,' because through you we draw down on ourselves the mercy and grace of our Lord" (Sullivan, *Correspondence* 461). Temporal existence is temporal, but with works of mercy it sparks an everlasting call to have Jesus become our eternal light in the darkest rooms of our own lives and the lives of others.

Even small gestures can help create communal bonds. Last year, with the approach of the Lenten season, I explained to my classes that during the days of Lent, I would grant something extra to my classes and not just deny myself certain edibles or comfort pleasures. I announced that at the beginning of each class, for a few minutes after prayer, they could ask me to do something for them that was not subject related. Suggestions of giving a hug, interpreting a short dream, a humorous excerpt from life etc., eventually became incorporated into the class atmosphere. It became a positive motivator because the students had a choice in the giving. To this day, I still have a student that sends me e-mail hugs. This small gesture during Lent that called us to a closer union with each other, formed for us, a stronger human bond. Being Catherine's light in the world brings to mind the "Prayer of Saint Francis of Assisi" where I am challenged to turn outward "to sow love", to bring light "where there is darkness" and to address our "Divine Master [to] grant that I may not so much seek…to be loved as to love. For it is in giving that we receive…."

In my teaching ministry, I have experienced 23 years of "receiving". The varied thank-yous that I have collected over the years have become living testimonials of Catherine's progressive presence in my ministry. In the first eleven years, I received acknowledgements of my basic talents with some sprinkling of spiritual potential but had only a peripheral understanding of Catherine McAuley's charism; however, it was in the last 12 years, that I witnessed her active presence. During this time, I felt intuitively guided by her commitment to compassion and unconditional love through a servant-like approach towards others. In those latter years of teaching, I began to understand what Jesus meant when He said to his disciples: "…the Son of man did not come to be served but to serve…" (Matthew 21:28). Catherine faithfully carried out this call of servanthood; she minimized the self to serve others unconditionally. In her approach to servanthood, she cautioned her followers "…[to] take care of the worm of good works which is vanity arising from self-approbation and esteem" (Sullivan, *Correspondence* 459).

The ego has a way of ensnaring us, tempting us into the human frailty of attributing the good that we do to our own power. When our response becomes self-centered, we lose sight of our primary source – God. Losing sight of God's will, makes us susceptible to self-error. In the Bible, Jesus even rebukes Peter for uttering his human concern about Jesus' upcoming suffering. Here Jesus is pointing out to all of us to be more aware of the ways of God rather than of man. He admonishes Peter: "You are an obstacle to me. You are thinking not as God does, but as human beings do" (Matthew 16:23). Catherine's whole life was a centering in God. In the Rule and Constitutions, Chapter 5, paragraph 4, she clearly states what should drive works of Mercy. Although it is addressed to the Sisters of Mercy, I think it is applicable to all who try to follow her view of self-discipline:

> The Sisters should consider purity of intention in all their works, not merely as a simple practice of piety, but as an essential duty of Religion. They shall therefore most studiously watch over themselves and guard against the insinuations of self-love, lest they lose the merit of their labors and good works by self complacency, vain glory, or by having in their actions any other motive, or end in view, than to please Almighty God. (Sullivan, *Catherine McAuley* 301)

In light of Catherine's way of life, I would like to share three glimpses of "living with Catherine McAuley" where I became an "unexpected receiver" of a Catherine McAuley Moment. These "Catherine glimpses" summarize the legacy of Catherine as it evolved during my teaching ministry. I think the following excerpts from past students can represent all Mercy students who have implanted into their own future a remnant of Catherine's vision through the Mercy education they have received. Catherine herself underscores the importance of a "careful instruction of women" so that they can be ready to meet the challenges of "the station they are destined to fill". Furthermore, Catherine states that this goal can be accomplished more beneficially "where ever a religious [believing] woman presides, [because] peace and good order are generally to be found [there]" (Sullivan, *Catherine McAuley* 297). Although I may have been a role model in the eyes of these students at the time, I became an "unexpected receiver" by trying to follow Catherine's call to teach with Mercy.

Excerpt from an e-mail received February 27, 2008 from Katie Metten, Class of 2000:

I was consistently challenged in your class. Your demeanor inspired girls to want to learn, want to do well, impress you, and work together. You are such a soft, kind person, but again, you portray an expectation that students behave in your classroom and respect you and one another. I will never forget the effect you and your classes had on me. You provoked a creativity inside of me that I still strive to satisfy today. I am 26, live in Houston, Texas and teach 4th grade in a public elementary school. I often think back to the way you made me feel in your class – safe, loved, equal, and capable of any challenge. Each day, I promise myself that I will do my best to make my students feel this way. If I can influence one life like you did mine – I will feel I have fulfilled God's role for me in life. I hope you know what a gift you have to teach young women, not only in your classroom, but in their lives beyond AHS. Thanks again for your commitment to education and the lives of young women like me!

Excerpt from letter received in my mailbox at school from Beth Robinson, Class of 2006:

Ulana M. Bochan

I hope you enjoyed your summer. I will be leaving on Saturday for college, but before I go, I wanted to write you a thank you. CP English was the hardest class that I took at Assumption, but it has also been the most beneficial so far. I want to thank you for pushing me to the limits of my ability. It has made lasting changes not only in my writing, but also in who I am as a person. Over the summer, I actually enjoyed analyzing and peer reviewing my friend's scholarship essay. Can you believe that? I even told her to include insight! In all seriousness I will tell you that I am taking my entire English binder with me to college. My Dad thinks I'm crazy, but I'm insisting on it. It wasn't just the course material that I will carry with me, but also the altered view of humanity.

I will never forget all the work we did on Ivan Denisovich and Night. I gained a fuller understanding of oppression and the human condition. You were gracious enough to share your own experiences which made the topic much more tangible and intense.

My last thank you has less to do with class and more with my senior retreat. I want to thank you for your talk on my senior retreat. My senior retreat was a very odd and at the same time, enlightening experience for me. Enlightening, because in only a few moments, my entire relationship with my Dad changed, and he wasn't even present. Many, many people have told me that my Dad means well and that he really loves me, but I never really saw it that way. I always thought that it was me against him. I had felt that way for a really long time, and after my Mom died, things completely deteriorated. I don't know exactly what it was about your talk that woke me up, but I did indeed wake up. The story you were telling wasn't really similar to mine, but as soon as you told it, I just thought, "Dad loves me, he loves me". That one moment has changed the course of my life. I understood then that we might never see eye to eye on anything but unconditional love, but the fact that unconditional love is there is enough. Once you helped me realize that, so many of the obstacles became insignificant, obsolete. For giving me that gift, one million thank yous could not be enough.

I'm not an overly superstitious person, but I do believe that some things happen for a reason and that people are in your life for a reason. I had you freshman year and senior year, full circle. You have been my teacher in every sense of the word. Thank you so much.

Excerpt from letter received in my mailbox from Lisa Sauer, Class of 2000:

Sometimes you meet a person who truly cares about others more than they will ever care about themselves. You can tell in the way they look at someone in need or the way they react in the instance that someone seeks help.

I remember when I had to go to a speech tournament and I was scared to death. I didn't feel prepared and since it was my first time going, I needed all of the help that I could get. You stayed after school for an hour listening to me recite my story. The amazing part was that you smiled every time (even though I knew after the fifth time it had probably lost its appeal). And then there's the time that you stopped me in the hall and told me I was doing a good job. I have never felt better. You have shown me what it means to be humble, what it means to be Christian, how to make someone feel good about herself, and you have shown me the type of person that I want to be when I grow up.

Thank you.

These particular acknowledgements bring Catherine McAuley to life because I felt I was guided by her vision of merciful outreach.

The pinnacle of "living with Catherine McAuley" happened to me the last year before I retired. I believe it was Catherine's doing to have the faculty choose me as "A Model of Mercy", one who attempts to emulate Catherine's vision in order to carry out the Mercy mission. This outward sign clearly indicated to me that having been immersed in her mission during my teaching years, I was not going to be able to let it go just because I was retiring. It had become a natural part of my identity. What started as a dim light has been enkindled into a bright light where I now can find my path better through prayer and good works. To retire, for me, now means to recycle the best that is in me into a needed direction.

I think Catherine's vision of compassion as a unifying force in the world is just as needed today as it was in the 19th century. Just looking at today's headlines creates a terrifying, unsettling atmosphere. Between crimes committed and natural disasters, a certain sense of helplessness can overpower our sincerest attempts if we are fueled only by our own power. However, if we are empowered by God as Catherine was, the "unbelievable" can happen through genuine empathy. In feeling compassion, we are driven to acts of love to follow Jesus' commandment to love one another and to know that "whatever [we do] for one of these least brothers [or sisters], we do for [Him]" (Matthew 25:40). Furthermore, when Jesus says: "Take my yoke upon you and learn from me, for I am meek and humble of heart" (Matthew 12:29), we can hear echoes of Catherine's commitment to totally embrace Jesus' invitation to come and follow Him. This beautiful invitation becomes the beating heart of Catherine's mission; for me, it becomes a life-long challenge, a goal to strive for.

I think I can venture to say that all of us who have embraced the Mercy mission can recognize what it means "to live with Catherine McAuley" in different forms and stages of our lives. These various stages of our lives allow us to experience our own Catherine McAuley Moments where our concrete giving of self illuminates a God-like quality of unconditional love at work. Catherine can be portrayed as a true disciple of Jesus; she welcomed "the stations of the cross" in her life with an unconditional love for all and a total reliance on God's Providence for the earthly work she needed to accomplish. I have "lived with Catherine McAuley" through my teaching ministry, experiencing God moments through Catherine's vision of merciful outreach.

In studying her life, I see how little I have done and how much more I can attempt to still do. I plan to continue my spiritual relationship with Catherine McAuley guided by her emphasis on prayer and service. It is in this spirit that I hope to fill my life with more Catherine McAuley Moments in this pilgrimage of one earthly life.

Works Cited

New American Bible. Wichita: Fireside Bible Publishers, 1994-1995 ed.

"Prayer of St. Francis". 2 April 2009

http://www.catholic-forum.com/saints/pray0027.htm

Regan, Joanna, RSM and Isabelle Keiss, RSM. *Tender Courage.* Chicago: Franciscan Herald Press, 1988.

Shakespeare, William. *Merchant of Venice.* 31 March 2009

http://shakespeare.mit.edu/merchant/merchant.4.1.html

Sullivan, Mary C., RSM. *Catherine McAuley and the Tradition of Mercy.* Notre Dame: University of Notre Dame Press, 1995, 2000.

Sullivan, Mary C., RSM, ed. *The Correspondence of Catherine McAuley. 1818-1841.* Washington: The Catholic University of America Press, 2004.

POINTS OF DEPARTURE

(Classroom Application)

Here is a suggested general outline for formative lesson plans based on each part of *Living with Catherine McAuley.*

Part I: Signposts

A. Teacher leads discussion of material in Part I and provides factual information about Catherine McAuley's signposts.

1. Students list their own individual signposts in any creative way.

    a. In groups of three, they share their creative signposts.

    b. Individually, they will present one signpost to the class.

    c. Then, they do an analysis of their own, looking for patterns, jotting down notes to be used in a writing assignment.

2. They write a paper that concentrates on the "now", using their analysis.

Part II: Values

A. Teacher leads discussion of material found in Part II and provides overall characteristics of Catherine McAuley's mission – building a value system.

1. Each student compiles a list of values from the Mercy tradition, choosing one or two she solidly believes in.

2. Teacher engages students in a Socratic Seminar to discuss values, applying them to Catherine and self.

3. Divide class members into groups according to values of interest.

4. Have them present an overview of this value based on Bible, literary sources, news, etc. defining it and stressing the importance of it.

5. Have them show how it fits into their lives, into communal bonding.

Part III: Challenge

A. After reading Part III, the teacher decides what background areas of Catherine's life still need to be explored such as social, economical, historical, philosophical, etc. and then solicits questions from class.

1. Teacher provides a short handout briefly defining these areas.

2. Based on areas of interest, teacher announces a Socratic Seminar.

3. From a list of Socratic Seminar topics, each student will choose one topic of interest to concentrate on.

B. The student will write a reactive paper based on facts which speculate how she would view Catherine's mission if she were placed in Catherine's time frame as either a friend or foe.

1. Students will share papers and discuss any pros or cons.

2. Students will round-up ideas in a concluding Socratic Seminar demonstrating an understanding of Catherine McAuley's biographical and spiritual profile.

Part IV: Catherine McAuley Moments

A. Teacher defines and explains Catherine McAuley Moments with examples of giving and receiving based on Part II and III and any personal examples.

1. Students write an assessment of what they have learned about Catherine McAuley in the classroom and experienced outside of the classroom.

2. The assessment should also include what value they will try to incorporate into their own lives.

3. As a conclusion, the teacher will host a tea party (according to the tradition of Catherine McAuley) and invite students to share their Catherine moments and create new ones as they continue to "Live with Catherine McAuley".